Paddleball and Racquetball

GOODYEAR
Physical Activities Series

Edited by J. Tillman Hall

Archery	Jean A. Barrett *California State University, Fullerton*
Badminton	James Poole *California State University, Northridge*
Bowling	Norman E. Showers *Southern Illinois University*
Fencing	Nancy L. Curry *Southwest Missouri State College*
Folk Dance	J. Tillman Hall *University of Southern California*
Golf	Edward F. Chui *University of Hawaii*
Handball	Pete Tyson *University of Texas*
Men's Basketball	Richard H. Perry *University of Southern California*
Men's Gymnastics	Gordon Maddux *California State University, Los Angeles*
Paddleball and Racquetball	A. William Fleming *Florida International University* Joel A. Bloom *University of Houston*
Soccer	John Callaghan *University of Southern California*
Social Dance	John G. Youmans *Temple University*

Swimming

Donald L. Gambril
Harvard University

**Fundamentals of
Physical Education**

J. Tillman Hall
University of Southern California

Kenneth C. Lersten
University of Southern California

Merril J. Melnick
University of Southern California

Talmage W. Morash
California State University, Northridge

Richard H. Perry
University of Southern California

Robert A. Pestolesi
California State University, Long Beach

Burton Seidler
California State University, Los Angeles

Volleyball

Randy Sandefur
California State University, Long Beach

Tennis

Barry C. Pelton
University of Houston

Women's Basketball

Ann Stutts
California State University, Northridge

Women's Gymnastics

Mary L. Schreiber
California State University, Los Angeles

GOODYEAR PUBLISHING COMPANY, INC.
Santa Monica, California 90401

Goodyear Physical Activities Series
J. Tillman Hall: *Series Editor*

A. William Fleming
Florida International University

Joel A. Bloom
University of Houston

Paddleball and Racquetball

Acknowledgments

I wish to thank the National Paddleball Association and the International Racquetball Association for their permission to reprint the NPA and IRA rules. Thanks also to the following individuals whose pictures appear in this book: Heather Fleming, Marjorie Fleming, Billy Jones, Larry Lopez and Tom Watson. Special appreciation is expressed to Bill Crevier for his fine photography.

Copyright © 1973 by
GOODYEAR PUBLISHING COMPANY, INC.
Santa Monica, California

Library of Congress Catalog Card Number: 72-90984

Current printing (last number):
10 9 8 7 6 5

ISBN: 0-87620-660-7
Y-6607-9
Printed in the United States of America

Contents

Editor's note

The Goodyear Publishing Company presents a series of physical education books written by instructors expert in their respective fields.

These books on major sports are intended as supplementary material for the instructors and to aid the student in the understanding and mastery of the sport of his choice. Each book covers its fundamentals, the beginning techniques, rules and customs, equipment, and terms and gives to the reader the spirit of the sport.

Each author of this series brings to the reader the knowledge and skill acquired over many years of teaching and coaching. We sincerely hope that these books will prove invaluable to the college student of the sport.

In paddleball and racquetball, William Fleming and Joel A. Bloom present a comprehensive analysis of the rules of the game, strategy for playing and all the basic strokes. The authors are expert players and have taught and coached successfully at Florida International University and the University of Houston. Racquetball is a rather new game and is currently being acclaimed as the test sport creation since World War II. The authors have presented an excellent approach on how to play this fast moving game.

The tear-out student/teacher evaluation forms included in this book should be a real asset to both the teacher and the student.

Preface

THE SPIN OF THE BALL

Many people use the terms paddle and racquetball synonymously; this is wrong. Paddleball is played with either a solid paddle or one with small holes bored in it to cut down air resistance, while racquetball is played with a strung (gut or nylon) racquet that is generally made of wood, steel or plastic. (See Fig. 1.) The difference between the two games lies in the area of what can be done to the ball with either the paddle or the racquet. The player using the racquet has the advantage, because of the strings, of being able to impart spin to the ball. In addition, because of less air resistance and the new light weight of the steel and plastic racquets, the racquetball player is able to hit the ball harder.

Fig. 2 illustrates the types of spin that can be put on the ball. The game of racquetball may require a bit more skill to become proficient at hitting the different shots and spins. Racquetball is probably the better game for women and girls (though they can play both and are becoming very good at them), because of the lighter weight of the racquet and the increased power that the strings afford them. There should be no difference between the way women and men play the games.

Figure 1 (A) A type of paddle (B) A type of racquet

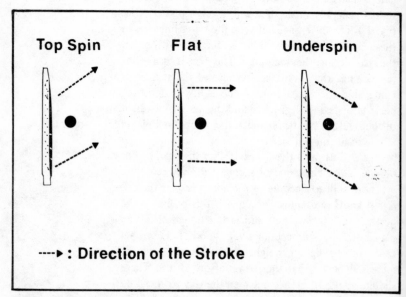

Figure 2 Types of spin

The advantages offered by paddleball are a slower game and perhaps a less complicated one due to less spin imparted to the ball. It is possible to impart spin to the ball with the paddle but not as much as with the racquet. The game is slower because more speed can be generated with the strung racquet; however, paddleball can still be a fast game. It may be a harder game on you physically because of the increased air resistance, the lack of give in the paddle, and the weight of the paddle.

You will probably want to try both games and will undoubtedly have a favorite. Remember that both games offer a tremendous opportunity for exercise, the development of skill, strength, stamina, sportsmanship, psychology, strategy and just plain enjoyment.

Figure 3 A game for all ages

History

Paddleball is truly a modern sport. It was developed in 1930 by Earl Riskey of the University of Michigan. He got the idea for the game while he watched tennis players using the University of Michigan handball courts to practice their strokes. This prompted him to develop a game which has become one of the leading recreational activities for men and women in the United States.

Riskey, an avid paddle tennis player, began the game with a paddle tennis paddle and a sponge rubber ball. The ball soon proved to be too heavy and was replaced by a standard tennis ball. This also proved to be too heavy, in addition to being hard to follow in the light-colored handball court. To remedy this situation, he soaked the balls in gasoline, removed their covers, and used the red rubber shells, which were much livelier and easier to follow.

The paddle also needed some modifications. When a player's hand perspired, the paddle frequently slipped from his grasp and endangered the other player or players in the court. To solve this problem, Riskey attached a rope loop to the paddle, which a player slipped over his wrist, thus preventing the loss of the paddle during play. Since Riskey developed his game in the handball court, he adapted the rules of that game to his.

During World War II, the Armed Forces adopted the game of paddleball as part of their conditioning program, which was held on the University of Michigan campus. As the men went on to other bases, they took the game with them and it spread further in popularity. Soon many recreation departments, YMCAs, Jewish Community Centers and schools began offering paddleball and the game was really on its way.

The National Paddleball Association was formed in 1952 with Earl Riskey as the first president, and from this organization and its leaders have come standardized rules, official equipment standards, and national tournaments. The first of these tournaments was held in 1961. The NPA has adopted the Pennsylvania 100 ball (the purple or grey ball with the pin hole through the surface), and the Marcraft 100 and 300 paddle models as their official equipment. There are other paddles available, however. The Official NPA Rules are available from the IM Sports Building, Ann Arbor, Michigan.

Racquetball is a game which developed as an offshoot of paddleball and has caught on tremendously in popularity. The exact origin of this game is rather uncertain; however, the most popular theory has it that some tennis players found their racquets were too long for safe, competitive use in a handball court, and so they simply cut the handles of old racquets down. They used these for play and found that the strings put greater action on the ball than did the flat paddle. They could also play a faster game.

Probably the greatest impetus to this form of the sport was the design of a racquet specifically for racquetball. Frames now come formed from wood, fiberglass, plastics and metal. The strings can be made from plastic, nylon, or gut. The choice of these materials is up to the individual player, as only the size of the racquet is prescribed by the rules. The International Racquetball Association was formed in 1968 by Bob Kendler and the United States Handball Association. There are now over 2,500 members active in the IRA, and because of its appeal to men and women alike it is growing tremendously. The International Racquetball Association has adopted the Seamless 558 (black) ball and the Sportcraft line of racquets as their official equipment; however, there are other racquets available. Official IRA tournaments were started and the first Open Singles Championship was won by Dr. Bud Muehleisen in 1969.

Racquetball rules are published through the International Racquetball Association and are available at most YMCAs, Jewish Community Centers, or through the IRA, 4101 Dempster St., Skokie, Illinois 60076.

Figure 1.1 Preparation for a forehand kill shot

Terminology
and
Etiquette

2

As an aspiring racquetball or paddleball player you must be as aware of the unwritten rules of the games as you are of the written ones. These unwritten rules are usually called etiquette and as you read, you will find that most of them are common sense.

The most important thing for you to consider and remember at all times is the object of the game: enjoyment. If you cannot have an enjoyable time playing the game you ought to question why you are pursuing it, instead of something else. With this in mind there are a number of things you can do to make your game and your opponent's more amicable.

When you make a date for a game be sure that you show up on time, but if you find you cannot be there or will be late, try to reach your opponent beforehand so you can both adjust your schedules.

As you begin the game of racquetball or paddleball and progress to different levels of skill, you will find opponents of varying degrees of skill. Try to pair yourself with someone of equal or slightly better ability. Remember, however, that you are going to learn more from the better players. Try not to force yourself on the best players, but if they ask you to play or join a doubles match consider it privilege and do your best to play and learn. Hopefully you will be in their position some day.

When you go to the courts to play or practice, make sure you are attired in the proper uniform and have the correct equipment. White is the only accepted color for official Paddleball matches while white, light, or bright colors are accepted for official Racquetball matches. The rules for both activities make no mention as to whether women should wear shorts or tennis dresses. Remember that since most of the courts are enclosed odors are greatly magnified. Therefore it is extremely important that you and your clothes be clean. Because the balls used in both games tend to break or split after a certain amount of use, it is a good idea to take an extra one with you to the court. You may also be wise to take an extra racquet or paddle with you, though they do not break very often. Include a towel with your equipment for the purpose of drying off, and also for wiping the floor in case of a fall or dripping perspiration.

Preparation for a game or match is important, and your warmup should accomplish this. As you warmup, either alone or with your opponent, be to start slowly so as to not pull any muscles or injure yourself. While warming up with your opponent try to spot any of his outstanding weaknesses or strengths. Be sure that you take an adequate warmup on all of the shots that you will use during the game and let your opponent do the same if he desires.

Once the match has begun there are a few things that you must do to insure that good sportsmanship will prevail and that injuries will be avoided. This is extremely important because of the relatively small, confined space in which the racquet or paddle is being swung, rather violently at times.

Prior to putting your serve in play always check to see that your opponent is ready and call out the score (calling your score first) before each serve. This will help avoid confusion with regard to the score, and the game will progress more smoothly. Try not to talk too much during the game, and especially while your opponent is making a shot. While playing doubles it is permissible and advisable to help one another out by calling for certain shots that you can take more easily than your partner, or vice versa.

Be fair on your calls and shots. Do not take advantage of your opponent on shots that he cannot see land or on shots that you did not execute legally. Remember that if you start taking unfair advantage, your opponent may do so also, or even worse, he may refuse to play with you and he could spread the word that you do not play fairly.

Avoid body contact at all times with your opponent. It is much easier to call a hinder and replay the point than to take a chance on making the shot and ending up with an injury. If you cannot make a return or shot without complete freedom of swing, call a hinder, rather than take a chance of hitting your opponent with your racquet or paddle. In between points, bounce the ball or hand the ball to your opponent — do not hit it at him.

Above all, control your temper! No one likes to play with a hot-tempered player or a bad sport. Banging your racquet or paddle against the walls or floor is expensive and dangerous, and has no place in the court. Swearing, shouting and grumbling only serve to upset you and your opponents. Try to remember that your main objective in playing racquetball and paddleball is enjoyment, then exercise and the improvement of your game. Have fun playing, and you will play better.

TERMINOLOGY

The following terms apply to both racquetball and paddleball. Most of the definitions are taken directly from the Official Paddleball Rules (see the list of suggested readings at the end of this book).

ACE   A serve untouched by the receiver.

BACK COURT   The area back of the short line.

BACKHAND   Hitting the ball from the side opposite the forehand.

BACKSWING   Taking the paddle back in preparation for beginning the swing.

BLOCKING   Preventing opponent from hitting ball by moving some part of body between opponent and ball.

CEILING SHOT   A shot that strikes the ceiling before hitting the front wall.

CENTER COURT   The area near the short line in the middle of the court.

COURT   The playing area.

COURT HINDER   An automatic hinder (if the local rules so specify) caused when the ball strikes a court construction obstacle such as a door latch.

CROTCH BALL   A ball hitting at the junction of the floor and a wall.

CUT-THROAT   A game involving three players with each player playing against the other two.

DEAD BALL   A ball which is no longer in play.

DEFENSIVE SHOT   A shot hit to maneuver an opponent into a position close to the back wall.

DOUBLES   Two players playing against two other players.

DRIVE   Hitting the ball hard to the front wall so that it rebounds on a relatively straight line.

ERROR   Failure to successfully return a ball hit during play.

FAULT   An infraction of the service rule.

FOLLOW THROUGH   The continuation of the swing of the paddle after the ball has been hit.

FOOT FAULT   Illegal position of the server's feet on the serve.

FRONT COURT   The court area in front of the service line.

GAME   The winning of twenty-one points which constitutes a game.

HALF-VOLLEY   Hitting the ball just after it bounces from the playing surface.

HAND OUT   The loss of service by the player on a doubles team who is the first server on that team.

HINDER   Unintentional interference with an opponent during play resulting in replay of point.

ILLEGAL SERVE   Failure to serve the ball in accordance with the playing rules.

KILL   A ball hit so low to the front wall that it is practically unplayable.

LOB   A ball hit high and gently to the front wall which rebounds in a high arc to the back wall.

LONG   A served ball that first hits the front wall and rebounds to the back wall before touching the floor. An illegal serve.

MATCH   The winning of two out of three games.

OVERHEAD   The racquet or paddle stroke used when hitting the ball from a shoulder-high or higher position.

PASS   A ball hit to the side and out of reach of an opponent.

PLACEMENT   A shot hit to the spot where it was intended, which cannot be returned.

POINT   A mark scored by the serving side or serving player.

RALLY   The playing time between the serve and the end of the point.

RECEIVER   The reciever of the serve.

REST PERIOD   Intervals during and between games in accordance with the rules.

SCREEN   Interference with opponent's vision in attempting to play the ball.

SERVE   The act of putting the ball into play.

SERVE OUT   A player losing serve in accordance with the rules.

SERVER   The player hitting the ball to the front wall to begin the play of the point.

SERVICE BOX   In doubles, the area in which the server's partner must remain until the serve has passed the short line.

SERVICE LINE   In four-wall racquetball or paddleball, a line parallel to and five feet in front of the short line. In one-wall racquetball or paddleball it is a line parallel to and nine feet back of the short line.

SERVICE ZONE   The area between and including the service line and the short line.

SHADOW SERVE   A served ball passing so close to the server's body on the rebound that the receiver is unable to pick up the flight of the ball.

SHORT   A serve failing to rebound past the short line.

SHORT LINE   In four-wall racquetball or paddleball, a line midway between and parallel with the front and back walls. In one-wall racquetball or paddleball, a line parallel to and sixteen feet from the front wall.

SIDE LINES   The lines marking left and right-hand boundaries of the court in one-wall and three-wall racquetball or paddleball.

SIDE OUT   Loss of service by a player in singles or both players in doubles.

SINGLES   The game of racquetball or paddleball played by two opposing players.

STRADDLEBALL   A ball going between the legs of a player.

VOLLEY   Playing the ball in the air before it has bounced.

Rules

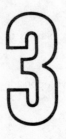

The following are the official rules for paddleball and racquetball as published by the National Paddleball Association and the International Racquetball Association respectively.

PADDLEBALL

Rule I – The Game

1. **Players**
   Paddleball may be played by two players (singles), three players (cut-throat), or four players (doubles).

2. **Description**
   The game is played with a wooden paddle and a paddleball in a four-wall, one-wall, or three-wall court.

3. **Game Score**
   A game is won by the side first scoring twenty-one points. Points are scored only by the serving side when it serves an ace or wins a volley.

4. **Match Score**
   A match consists of the best two out of three games.

Rule II – Court

1. **Four-Wall**
   The standard four-wall court is 40 feet long, 20 feet wide with front and sidewalls 20 feet high, a back wall at least 12 feet high, and a ceiling. A line midway between and parallel with the front and back walls divides the court in the center and is called the *short line*. A line five feet in front of the short line and parallel to it is called the *service line*. The space between and including these two lines is called the *service zone*. A line 18 inches from and parallel with the sidewall at each end of the service zone is called the service box. All lines are 1½ inches wide and are red or black.

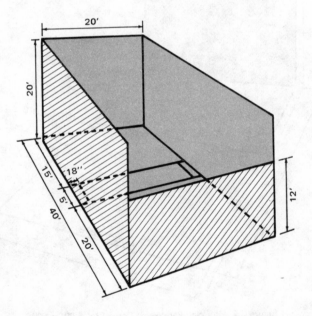

Figure 3.1 Four-Wall Paddleball Court (40' x 20' x 20')

2. **One-Wall**
   The standard one-wall court is 34 feet long and 20 feet wide with a front wall which is 16 feet high and 20 feet wide with a 4-foot wire fence running along the top of the front wall. A line 16 feet from the front wall and running parallel with the front wall between the

sidelines is called the short line. Nine feet behind the short line and parallel to it are lines at least six inches long on either side of the court which are called service lines. The area between these service lines and the short line is the service zone. Each sideline is extended three feet beyond the end line to assist players and officials in determining long balls and serve-outs on the same serve. All lines are 1½ inches wide. There should be a playing space of at least six feet on either side and behind the court.

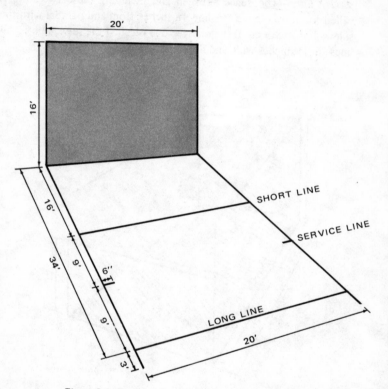

Figure 3.2 One-Wall Paddleball Court (34′ x 20′ x 16′)

3. **Three-Wall**

The standard three-wall court is the same as the one-wall court with the exception of having a wall extend from the top of the front wall back along either sideline and slanting downward to a height of six feet at the short line at which point it stops. All other dimensions are the same.

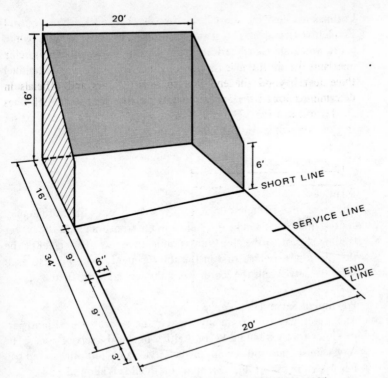

Figure 3.3 Three-Wall Paddleball Court (34' x 20' x 16')

Rule III — Equipment

1. **Paddle**
   The official paddle is wooden and is approximately 8 inches wide, 16 inches long, weighing approximately 16 ounces, with a leather thong attached to the end of the handle, which must be worn around the wrist during play. Racquets with strings are not permitted. (An "official" paddle is manufactured by Marcraft Recreation, Inc., 305 East 140th St., Bronx, N. Y. 10454.)

2. **Ball**
   The official paddleball is the Pennsy Official National Paddleball made by General Tire-Pennsylvania Athletic Products, Akron, Ohio. When dropped from a height of 6 feet it should rebound approximately 3½ feet. Balls shall be approved for play by the referee prior to the start of the match.

3. **Uniform**

    For tournament play players are required to wear white shirts, white socks, white shorts and white shoes. A team name or club insignia may be worn on the shirt. A glove may be worn on the hand holding the paddle. Knee and elbow pads of a soft material may be worn. Warm-up suits, if worn in a match, must also be white.

Rule IV — Serving Regulations

1. **Serve**

    The serve shall be determined by a toss fo a coin. In informal play contestants can rebound the ball from the front wall with the player landing closest to the short line winning the serve. The server of the first game also serves first in the third game, if any. Prior to each serve the server calls the score, giving the server's score first.

2. **Position of Server** (Four-Wall)

    The server may serve from anywhere in the service zone with no part of either foot extending *beyond* either line of the service zone. The server must start and remain in the service zone until the served ball has passed the short line. Stepping on the line is allowed.

3. **Position of Server** (One and Three-Wall)

    The server may serve from anywhere in the service zone between the short line and service lines with no part of either foot extending *be yond* either line of the service zone. The server must start and remain in the service zone until the served ball has returned beyond the short line. Stepping on the line is permitted.

4. **Violation**

    A violation of the serve is called a foot fault and is an illegal serve. Two illegal serves in succession result in a serve-out.

5. **Method of Serving** (Four-Wall)

    The ball must be dropped to the floor within the service zone and struck with the paddle on the first bounce, hitting the front wall first and rebounding back of the short line, either with or without touching one sidewall. The server shall not serve until his opponent is ready.

6.   **Method of Serving** (One-Wall)
     The ball must be dropped to the playing surface within the service zone and struck with the paddle on the first bounce, hitting the front wall first and rebounding back of the short line, and within or on either side line or the back line. The server shall not serve until his opponent is ready.

7.   **Method of Serving** (Three-Wall)
     Same as one-wall except that in three-wall the ball may legally touch one side wall after hitting the front wall.

8.   **Service in Doubles**
     In doubles the side starting each game is allowed only one serve-out. Thereafter, in that game, both players on each side are permitted to serve until a serve-out occurs. The service order established at the beginning of each game must be followed throughout that game. Servers do not have to alternate serves to their opponents. Serving out of order or the same player serving both serves is a serve-out.

9.   **Partner's Position** (Four-Wall)
     During the serve the server's partner is required to stand within the service box with his back against the wall and both feet on the floor until the ball passes the short line. Failure to take this position during a serve is a foot fault. If, while in legal position, a player is hit by a served ball on the fly it is a dead ball giving the server another serve. If hit by the serve when out of the box it is a serve-out. A ball passing behind a player legally in the box is a hinder. A dead ball serve does not eliminate a previous fault on that particular service.

10. **Partner's Position** (One and Three-Wall)
     During the serve the server's partner is required to stand outside the sideline between the short line and back line until the ball passes the short line. Failure to take this position during a serve is a foot fault. If the server's partner enters the playing area between the sidelines before the served ball passes him, it is a fault.

11. **Illegal Serves** (Four-Wall)
     Any two illegal serves in succession put the server out. An illegal serve cannot be played. The following are illegal serves:
     a.   **Short Serve** — A served ball which hits the floor before crossing the short line.

b.   **Long Serve** — A served ball rebounding from the front wall to the back wall before hitting the floor.

c.   **Ceiling Serve** — A served ball rebounding from the front wall and hitting the ceiling before hitting the floor.

d.   **Two-side Serve** — A served ball rebounding from the front wall and hitting two or more walls before hitting the floor.

e.   **Out of Court Serve** — A served ball going out of the court.

f.   **Foot Fault** — The server stepping out of or leaving the service zone before the ball passes the short line or server's partner in doubles, not staying in service box as required.

12. **Serve-out Serves (Four-Wall)**
The following "out serves" result in a serve-out:

a.   Bouncing the ball more than twice before striking it when in the act of serving.

b.   Bouncing the ball and having it hit the sidewall.

c.   Dropping the ball and hitting it in the air (accidentally dropping the ball does not put the server out).

d.   Striking at and missing the dropped serve.

e.   Touching the server's body or clothing with the ball in the act of serving.

f.   Any serve which simultaneously strikes the front wall and the floor, ceiling, or sidewall.

13. **Illegal Serves (One and Three-Wall)**
Any two illegal serves in succession put the server out. An illegal serve cannot be played. The following are illegal serves:

a.   **Short Serve** — A served ball which hits the playing surface before crossing the short line.

b.   **Long Serve** — A served ball rebounding from the front wall beyond the end line between the sidelines extended before hitting the playing surface.

c.   **Foot Fault** — The server stepping out of or leaving the service zone before the ball passes the short line or server's partner in doubles, not staying outside the service area as required.

d.   **Three-Wall** — In three-wall any serve which strikes the front wall and two sidewalls before hitting the playing surface.

14. **Serve-outs (One and Three-Wall)**
The following "out servers" result in a serve-out:

a.   Bouncing the ball more than twice before striking it when in the act of serving.

b.   Dropping the ball and hitting it in the air (accidentally dropping the ball does not put the server out).

c.   Striking at and missing the dropped serve.

d.   Touching the server's body or clothing with the ball in the act of serving.

e.   Any serve which simultaneously strikes the front wall and the playing surface.

f.   In three-wall, any serve striking the sidewall before the front wall.

Rule V — Playing Regulations

1.   **Return of Service (Four-Wall)**

a.   The receiver(s) must remain at least five feet back of the short line until the ball is struck by the server.

b.   A legally served ball must be returned on the fly or after the first bounce to the front wall either directly or after touching the sidewall(s), ceiling, or back wall. A return touching the front wall and floor simultaneously is not a good return.

c.   In returning a service on the fly, no part of the receiver's body may cross the short line before making the return.

d.   Failure to legally return the service results in a point for the server.

2.   **Return of Service (One and Three-Wall)**

a.   The receiver(s) must stand back of the service line until the ball passes the short line.

b.   A legally served ball must be returned on the fly or after the first bounce to the front wall. A return touching the front wall and playing surface simultaneously is not a good return.

c.   In returning a service on the fly no part of the receiver's body may cross the short line before making the return.

d.   Failure to legally return the service results in a point for the server.

3.   **Playing the Ball**

A legal return of service or of an opponent's shot is called a volley. The following rules must be observed. Failure to do so results in a serve-out or point.

a.   The ball must be hit with the paddle in one or both hands. The safety thong must be around the wrist at all times.

b. Hitting the ball with the arm, hand, or any part of the body is prohibited.

c. In attempting a return the ball may be touched only once. If a player swings at the ball but misses it, he or his partner in doubles may make a further attempt to return it until it touches the floor a second time.

d. In doubles both partners may swing at and simultaneously strike a ball.

e. Any ball struck at in play which goes out of court or which is returned to the front wall and then on the rebound or on the first bounce goes out of court is a serve-out or point.

4. **Unintentional Hinders (Point Replayed)**
It is a hinder if a player unintentionally interferes with an opponent preventing him from having a fair opportunity to hit the ball. Each player must get out of his opponent's way immediately after he has struck the ball and

a. must give his opponent a fair opportunity to get to and/or strike at the ball. If a player in attempting to get into position goes in the wrong direction and his opponent stands still this does *not* constitue a hinder.

b. must give his opponent a fair view of the ball provided, however, interference with his opponent's vision in following the flight of the ball is *not* a hinder.

c. must allow his opponent an opportunity to play the ball from any part of the court.

d. must allow his opponent to play the ball to any part of the front wall and to either sidewall or the back wall in three and four-wall courts.

e. unnecessary interference with an opponent or unnecessary crowding, even through the opposing player is not actually prevented from reaching or striking the ball, is a hinder.

5. **Other Unintentional Hinders**
a. A returned ball striking an opponent on the fly on its return to the front wall.

b. Hitting any part of the court that under local rules is a dead ball.

c. A ball rebounding irom the front wall on the serve so close to the body of the server that the opponent is interfered with or prevented from seeing the ball. (Called a shadow ball.)

d. A ball going between the legs of a player on the side which just returned the ball so that the opponent does not have a fair chance to see or return the ball. (Called a straddle ball.)

e. Body contact with an opponent which interferes with his seeing or returning the ball.

f. Any other unintentional interference that prevents an opponent from seeing or returning the ball.

g. It is not a hinder when a player hinders his partner.

h. A player is not entitled to a hinder unless the interference occurred before or simultaneously with his paddle's contact with the ball.

6. **Intentional Hinder (Serve-out or Point)**

a. A player failing to move sufficiently to allow his opponent a fair shot.

b. Intentionally pushing an opponent during a play.

c. Blocking the movement of an opponent by moving into his path.

7. **Wet Ball**
On the service and during play the ball and the paddle must be dry.

8. **Replay of Point**
Any foreign object entering the court or any other outside interference causes play to stop and the point is replayed.

9. **Broken Ball**
If a ball breaks during play the point is replayed.

10. **Rest Periods Between Games**
A two-minute rest period is allowed between games one and two. Players are not permitted to leave the court. A ten-minute rest period is allowed between the second third game during which time players are allowed to leave the court.

11. **Continuity of Play**
Play shall be continuous from the first serve of each game until the game is concluded except that during a game each player in singles, or each side in doubles, either during serving or receiving, may request a time-out not to exceed thirty seconds. No more than two time-outs per game shall be allowed each player or each team in

doubles. Deliberate delay shall result in a point or side-out against the offender.

12. **Safety**
The safety thong must be around the wrist at all times. The paddle may not be switched from one hand to the other. Both hands on the paddle together may be used in striking the ball.

13. **Injuries**
Play may be suspended for up to 15 minutes for an injury. If the injured player is unable to continue the match is forfeited. If the match is resumed and must then be stopped again for the same player the match is forfeited.

14. Prior to each serve the server should call the score, giving the server's score first.

Rule VI – Officiating

All tournament matches should be conducted with a referee and scorer whose duties are as follows:

Referee:
1. Brief all players and officials on the rules and local playing regulations.
2. Check the playing area for suitability for play.
3. Check the playing equipment and uniform of players and approve of same.
4. Check availability of other necessary equipment such as extra balls, towels, scorecards, pencils.
5. Introduce players, toss coin for choice of serving or receiving.
6. Take position in center and above the back wall of the back court and signal start of game.
   Note: In a three-wall match referee's position is at the side of the court near where the sidewall ends. In a one-wall match referee's position is on the side and toward the front of the court on an elevated platform.
7. During game decide on all questions that arise in accordance with the rules. He is responsible for the entire conduct of the game including:
   a. legality of the serve and its return.
   b. calling of unintentional hinders, intentional hinders and faults.

     c.   preventing any unnecessary delay during match.
     d.   announcing when a point is made or server is out.
     e.   deciding on all questions in accordance with the rules and all
           questions not covered by the rules.
     f.   forfeiting or postponing a match at his discretion.

8. Matches may be forfeited when:
     a.   A player refuses to abide by the referee's decision.
     b.   A player fails to appear for a scheduled contest within 15
           minutes.
     c.   A player is unable to continue play for physical reasons.

9. The decision of the referee is final.

10. Approve the final score after announcing the name of the winner of
    the match and the scores of all games played.
    Scorer:
1. Assist referee in prematch responsibilities.
2. Obtain necessary equipment for scoring match including scorecard,
    pencils, extra balls, towels, etc.
3. Assist the referee in any and all capacities at the referee's discretion.
4. Keep a record of the progress of the game as prescribed by the
    tournament committee.
*5. Keep players and spectators informed on the progress of the game by
    announcing score after each exchange. The scorecard should then
    be given to the referee for his approval.

Note: Referee may assume the responsibility for announcing running
game score.

OFFICIAL ONE-WALL PADDLEBALL RULES

The U.S. Paddleball Association, chaired by Chris Lecakes, conducts
yearly one-wall tournaments in the New York area. The court is the same
dimensions as that used by the NPA for one-wall paddleball, and many of
the rules are the same.

Exceptions to the NPA rules are listed below:

Scoring:

1. A point is scored for each and every out of the game. It is not neces-
    sary for a side to be serving in order to score a point.

2.   Both partners of a side shall serve in succession. The first server shall retain his serve until his side loses one point. His partner shall than serve. Upon loss of the next point, the opposing team shall serve.

3.   A game is ended at 25 points unless both sides tie at 24 points. In this case, the game must be won by a two point margin, i.e., 26-24, 28-26, etc. . . .

4.   Any combination of two faults shall retire the server and score a points for the opponents(s).

The Serve:

1.   Bouncing the ball more than 3 times in the service area before the serve is a fault.

2.   In singles, the server may serve from any part of the court within the service area (between the short line and service markets), and must serve to the major area of the court. If serving from the left side of the court, the ball must return to his right. If serving from the right side of the court, the ball must return to his left. If serving from the center of the court, the ball may return on either the right or left of the server, but the server must point out to his opponent as to which side of the court the serve shall go. Neglect by the server to notify his opponent of this is a fault.

3.   Should the serve land anywhere other than the major area of the court, it shall be a fault.

4.   Once the server elects to serve from a particular area of the court within the service zone, should he commit a hinder, fault, short or long, he must complete his serve from the area he has chosen.

Process of Play

1.   A player is allowed to switch the paddle from one hand to another during play.

2.   If, during play, a player hits a ball and, after striking the wall, passes one or both opponents in such a way as to make it impossible to return, and then in turn touches the striker or his partner, the point

shall go to the side hitting the ball. If there is any doubt by the referee as to whether or not the ball could possibly have been returned, the point shall be played over. Should the ball pass one or both opponents on the fly and then touch the striker or his partner, the referee shall rule whether or not the ball would have landed fair or out, or if the point should be played over.

3.   A player or side is entitled to two (separate) one minute time outs in any one game.

4.   A 5 minute rest period is allowed between the first and second game.

RACQUETBALL

FOUR–WALL RACQUETBALL RULES

Part 1. The Game

1.1   **Types of Games.** Racquetball may be played by two or four players. When played by two it is called "singles," and when played by four, "doubles."

1.2   **Description.** Racquetball, as the name implies, is a competitive game in which a racquet is used to serve and return the ball.

1.3   **Objective.** The objective is to win each volley by serving or returning the ball so the opponent is unable to keep the ball in play. A serve or volley is won when a side is unable to return the ball before it touches the floor twice.

1.4   **Points and Outs.** Points are scored only by the serving side when it serves an ace or wins a volley. When the serving side loses a volley it loses the serve. Losing the serve is called an "out" in singles, and a "handout" in doubles.

1.5   **Game.** A game is won by the side first scoring 21 points.

1.6   **Match.** A match is won by the side first winning two games.

Part II. Courts and Equipment

2.1   **Courts.** The specifications for the standard four-wall racquetball court are:

(a) **Dimension.** The dimensions shall be 20 feet wide, 20 feet high, and 40 feet long, with back wall at least 12 feet high.

(b) **Lines and Zones.** Racquetball courts shall be divided and marked on the floors with 1½ inch wide red or white lines as follows:

(c) **Short Line.** The short line is midway between and is parallel with the front and back walls dividing the court into equal front and back courts.

    (1) **Service Line.** The service line is parallel with and located 5 feet in front of the short line.

    (2) **Service Zone.** The service zone is the space between the outer edges of the short and service lines.

    (3) **Service Boxes.** A service box is located at each end of the service zone by lines 18 inches from and parallel with each side wall.

    (4) **Receiving Lines.** Five feet back of the short line, vertical lines shall be marked on each side wall extending 3 inches from the floor. See rule 4.7(a).

2.2 **Ball Specifications.** The specifications for the standard racquetball are:

(a) **Official Ball.** IRA.s official ball in the black Seamless 588. The ball shall be 2¼ inches in diameter; weight approximately 1.40 ounces with a bounce at 65-70 inches from 100 inch drop at a temperature of 76 degrees F.

2.3 **Ball Selection.** A new ball shall be selected by the referee for use in each match in all tournaments. During a game the referee may, at his discretion or at the request of both players or teams, select another ball. Balls that are not round or which bounce erratically shall not be used. The Seamless 558 ball is official for all IRA sanctioned tournaments.

2.4 **Racquet Specifications.** The specifications for the standard racquetball racquet are:

(a) **Official Racquet.** IRA's official racquets are the Sportcraft 13178 and 13188 (wood frames), 13175 (aluminum frame), and 13185 (steel frame).

(b) **Dimensions.** The Official racquet will have a maximum head length of 11 inches and a width of 9 inches. These measurements are computed from the outer edge of the racquet head rims. The handle may not exceed 7 inches in length. Total length and width of the racquet may not exceed a total of 27 inches.

(c) The racquet must include a thong that must be securely wrapped on the player's wrist.

(d) The racquet frame may be made on any material, as long as it conforms to the above specifications.

(e) The strings of the racquet must be gut, monofilament, or nylon, but cannot be of steel or metal.

2.5 **Uniform.** All parts of the uniform, consisting of a shirt, shorts, socks and shoes, shall be clean and light or bright in color. Warmup shirts and pants, if worn in actual match play, shall also be white, light or bright but may be of any color if not used in actual match play. In IRA-sanctioned tournaments, the tournament chairman or his delegated representative shall instruct doubles teams to wear uniforms of a different color. Only club insignia and/or name of club or racquetball organization may be on the uniform. Players may not play without shirts.

Part III. Officiating

3.1 **Tournaments.** All tournaments shall be managed by a committee or chairman, who shall designate the officials.

3.2 **Officials.** The officials shall include a referee and a scorer. Additional assistants and record keepers may be designated as desired.

3.3 **Qualifications.** Since the quality of the officiating often determines the success of each tournament, all officials shall be experienced or trained, and shall be thoroughly familiar with these rules and with the local playing conditions.

3.4 **Rule Briefing.** Before all tournaments, all officials and players shall be briefed on rules and on local court hinders or other regulations.

3.5 **Referees.**
(a) **Pre-Match Duties.** Before each match commences, it shall be the duty of the referee to:
(1) Check on adequacy of preparation of the court with respect to cleanliness, lighting and temperature, and upon

location of locker rooms, drinking fountains, etc.

(2) Check on availability and suitability of all materials necessary for the match such as balls, towels, score cards and pencils.

(3) Check readiness and qualifications of assisting officials.

(4) Explain court regulations to players and inspect the compliance of racquets with rules.

(5) Remind players to have an extra supply of adequate racquets and uniforms.

(6) Introduce players, toss coin, and signal start of first game.

(b) **Decisions.** During games the referee shall decide all questions that may arise in accordance with these rules. If there is body contact on the back swing, the player should call it quickly. This is the only call a player may make. On all questions involving judgment and on all questions not covered by these rules, the decision of the referee is final.

(c) **Protests.** Any decision not involving the judgement of the referee may on protest be decided by the chairman, if present, or his delegated representative.

(d) **Forfeitures.** A match may be forfeited by the referee when:

(1) Any player refuses to abide by the referee's decision, or engages in unsportsmanlike conduct.

(2) After warning, any player leaves the court without permission of the referee either during a game or between the first and second games.

(3) Any player for a singles match, or any team for a doubles match fails to report to play. Normally, 20 minutes from the scheduled game time will be allowed before forfeiture. The tournament chairman may permit a longer delay if circumstances warrant such a decision.

(4) If both players for a singles, or both teams for doubles fail to appear to play for consolation matches or other play-offs, they shall forfeit their ratings for future tournaments, and forfeit any trophies, medals, or awards.

3.6 **Scores.** The scorer shall keep a record of the progress of the game in the manner prescribed by the committee or chairman. As a minimum the progress record shall include the order of serves, outs, and points. The referee or scorer shall announce the score before each serve.

3.7 **Record Keepers.** In addition to the scorer, the committee may designate additional persons to keep more detailed records for statistical pruposes of the progress of the game.

Part IV. Play Regulations

4.1 **Serve-Generally**
   (a) **Order.** The player or side winning the toss becomes the first server and starts the first game, and the third game, if any.
   (b) **Start.** Games are started by the referee calling "play ball."
   (c) **Place.** The server may serve from any place in the service zone. No part of either foot may extend beyond either line of the service zone. Stepping on the line (but not beyond it) is permitted. Server must remain in the service zone until the served ball passes short line. Violations are called "foot faults."
   (d) **Manner.** A serve is commenced by bouncing the ball to the floor in the service zone, and on the first bounce the ball is struck by the server's racquet so that it hits the front wall and on the rebound hits the floor back of the short line, either with or without touching one of the side walls.
   (e) **Readiness.** Serves shall not be made until the receiving side is ready, or the referee has called play ball.

4.2 **Serve-In Doubles.**
   (a) **Server.** At the beginning of each game in doubles, each side shall inform the referee of the order of service, which order shall be followed throughout the game. Only the first server serves the first time up and continues to serve first throughout the game. When the first server is out — the side is out. Thereafter both players on each side shall serve until a hand-out occurs. It is not necessary for the server to alternate serves to their opponents.
   (b) **Partner's Position.** On each serve, the server's partner shall stand erect with his back to the side wall and with both feet on the floor within the service box until the served ball passes the short line. Violations are called "foot faults."

4.3 **Defective Serves.** Defective serves are of three types resulting in penalties as follows:
   (a) **Dead Ball Serve.** A dead ball serve results in no penalty and the server is given another serve without cancelling a prior illegal serve.

    (b)   **Fault Serve.** Two fault serves results in a hand-out.

    (c)   **Out Serves.** An out serve results in a hand-out.

4.4   **Dead Ball Serves.** Dead ball serves do not cancel any previous illegal serve. They occur when an otherwise legal serve:

    (a)   **Hits Partner.** Hits the server's partner on the fly on the rebound from the front wall while the server's partner is in the service box. Any serve that touches the floor before hitting the partner in the box is a short.

    (b)   **Screen Balls.** Passes too close to the server or the server's partner to obstruct the view of the returning side. Any serve passing behind the server's partner and the side wall is an automatic screen.

    (c)   **Court Hinders.** Hits any part of the court than under local rules is a dead ball.

4.5   **Fault Serves.** The following serves are faults and any two in succession results in a hand-out:

    (a)   **Foot Faults.** A foot fault results:

        (1)   When the server leaves the service zone before the served ball passes the short line.

        (2)   When the server's partner leaves the service zone before the served ball passes the short line.

    (b)   **Short Serve.** A short serve is any served ball that first hits the front wall and on the rebound hits the floor in front of the back edge of the short line either with or without touching one side wall; or

    (c)   **Three-Wall Serve.** A two-side serve is any ball served that first hits the front wall and on the rebound hits two side walls on the fly.

    (d)   **Ceiling Serve.** A ceiling serve is any served ball that touches the ceiling after hitting the front wall either with or without touching one side wall.

    (e)   **Long Serve.** A long serve is any served ball that first hits the front wall and rebounds to the back wall before touching the floor.

    (f)   **Out of Court Serve.** Any ball going out of the court on the serve.

4.6   **Out Serves.** Any one of the following serves results in a hand-out:

    (a)   **Bounces.** Bouncing the ball more than three times while in the service zone before striking the ball. One bounce is counted each time the ball hits the floor within the service zone. Once the server is within the service zone and the receiver is ready, the ball may not be bounced anywhere but on the floor within the service zone. Accidental dropping of the ball counts as one bounce.

(b) **Missed Ball.** Any attempt to strike the ball on the first bounce that results either in a total miss or in touching any part of the server's body other than his racquet.

(c) **Non-front Serve.** Any served ball that strikes the server's partner, or the ceiling, floor or side wall, before striking the front wall.

(d) **Touched Serve.** Any served ball that on the rebound from the front wall touches the server, or touches the server's partner while any part of his body is out of the service box, or the server's partner intentionally catches the served ball on the fly.

(e) **Out-of-Order Serve.** In doubles, when either partner serves out of order. Any points which may have been scored during an out-of-order serve will be automatically void with the score reverting to the score prior to the out-of-order serve.

(f) **Crotch Serve.** If the served ball hits the crotch in the front wall it is considered the same as hitting the floor and is an out. A crotch serve into the back wall is good and in play.

4.7   **Return of Serve.**

(a) **Receiving Position.** The receiver or receivers must stand at least 5 feet back of the short line, as indicated by the 3 inch verticle line on each side wall, and cannot return the ball until it passes the short line. Any infraction results in a point for the server.

(b) **Defective Serve.** To eliminate any misunderstanding the receiving side should not catch or touch a defectively served ball until called by the referee or it has touched the floor for the second time.

(c) **Fly Return.** In making a fly return, no part of the receiver's body or racquet may enter into the service zone. A violation by a receiver results in a point for the server.

(d) **Legal Return.** After the ball is legally served, one of the players on the receiving side must strike the ball with his racquet either on the fly or after the first bounce and before the ball touches the floor the second time to return the ball to the front wall either directly or after touching one or both side walls, the back wall or the ceiling, or any combination of those surfaces. A returned ball may not touch the floor before touching the front wall.

(1) It is legal to return the ball by striking the ball into the back wall first, then hitting the front wall on the fly or after hitting the side wall or ceiling.

(e) **Failure to Return.** The failure to return a serve results in a point for the server.

4.8 **Changes of Serve.**

(a) **Hand-out.** A server is entitled to continue serving until:

(1) **Out Serve.** He makes an out serve under Rule 4.6 or;

(2) **Fault Serves.** He makes two fault serves in succession under Rule 4.5, or;

(3) **Hits Partner.** He hits his partner with an attempted return before the ball touches the floor a second time.

(4) **Return Failure.** He or his partner fails to keep the ball in play by retruning it as required by Rule 4.7(d).

(5) **Avoidable Hinder.** He or his partner commits an avoidable hinder under Rule 4.11.

(b) **Side-out.**

(1) **In Singles.** In singles, retiring the server retires the side.

(2) **In Doubles.** In doubles, the side is retired when both partners have been put out, except on the first serve as provided in Rule 4.2(a).

(c) **Effect.** When the server or the side loses the serve, the server or serving side shall become the receiver; and the receiving side, the server; and so alternately in all subsequent services of the game.

4.9 **Volleys.** Each legal return after the serve is called a volley. Play during volleys shall be according to the following rules:

(a) **One or Both Hands.** Only the head of the racquet may be used at any time to return the ball. The ball must be hit with the racquet in one or both hands. Switching hands to hit a ball is out. The use of any portion of the body is an out.

(b) **One Touch.** In attempting returns, the ball may be touched only once by one player on the returning side. In doubles both partners may swing at, but only one, may hit the ball. Each violation of (a) or (b) results in a hand-out or point.

(c) **Return Attempts.**

    (1) **In Singles.** In singles, if a player swings at but misses the ball in play, the player may repeat his attempts to return the ball until it touches the floor the second time.

    (2) **In Doubles.** In doubles if one player swings at but misses the ball, both he and his partner may make further attempts to return the ball until it touches the floor the second time. Both partners on a side are entitled to an attempt to return the ball.

    (3) **Hinders.** In singles or doubles, if a player swings at but misses the ball in play, and in his, or his partner's attempt again to play the ball there is an unintentional interference by an opponent it shall be a hinder. (See Rule 4.10)

(d) **Touching Ball.** Except as provided in Rule 4.10, (a)(2), any touching of a ball before it touches the floor the second time by a player other than the one making a return is a point or out against the offending player.

(e) **Out of Court Ball.**

    (1) **After Return.** Any ball returned to the front wall which on the rebound or on the first bounce goes into the gallery or through any opening in a side wall shall be declared dead and the serve replayed.

    (2) **No Return.** Any ball not returned to the front wall, but which caroms off a player's racquet into the gallery or into any opening in a side wall either with or without touching the ceiling, side or back wall, shall be an out or point against the players failing to make the return.

(f) **Dry Ball.** During the game and particularly on service every effort should be made to keep the ball dry. Deliberately wetting shall result in an out. The ball may be inspected by the referee at any time during a game.

(g) **Broken Ball.** If there is any suspicion that a ball has broken on the serve or during a volley, play shall continue until the end of the volley. The referee or any player may request the ball be examined. If the referee decides the ball is broken or otherwise defective, a new ball shall be put into play and the point replayed.

(h) **Play Stoppage.**

    (1) If a player loses a shoe or other equipment, or foreign objects enter the court, or any other outside interference

occurs, the referee shall stop the play.

(2)   If a player loses control of his racquet, time should be called after the point has been decided, providing the racquet does not strike an opponent or interfere with ensuing play.

4.10 **Dead Ball Hinders.** Hinders are of two types — "dead ball" and "avoidable." Dead ball hinders as described in this rule results in the point being replayed. Avoidable hinders are described in Rule 4.11.

(a)   **Situations.** When called by the referee, the following are dead ball hinders:

(1)   **Court Hinders.** Hits any part of the court which under local rules is a dead ball.

(2)   **Hitting Opponent.** Any returned ball that touches an opponent on the fly before it returns to the front wall.

(3)   **Body Contact.** Any body contact with an opponent that interferes with seeing or returning ball.

(4)   **Screen Ball.** Any ball rebounding from the front wall close to the body of a player on the side which just returned the ball, to interfere with or prevent the returning side from seeing the ball. See Rule 4.4(b).

(5)   **Straddle Ball.** A ball passing between the legs of a player on the side which just returned the ball, if there is no fair chance to see or return the ball.

(6)   **Other Interference.** Any other unintentional interference which prevents an opponent from having a fair chance to see or return the ball.

(b)   **Effect.** A call by the referee of a "hinder" stops the play and voids any situation following, such as the ball hitting a player. No player is authorized to call a hinder, except on the back swing and such a call must be made immediately as provided in Rule 3.5(b).

(c)   **Avoidance.** While making an attempt to return the ball, a player is entitled to a fair chance to see and return the ball. It is the duty of the side that has just served or returned the ball to move so that the receiving side may go straight to the ball and not be required to go around an opponent. The referee should be liberal in calling hinders to discourage any practice of playing the ball where an adversary cannot see it until too late. It is no excuse that the ball is "killed," unless in the opinion of the referee the ball could not be returned. Hinders should be called without a claim by a player, especially in close playes and on game points.

(d) **In Doubles.** In doubles, both players on a side are entitled to a fair and unobstructed chance at the ball and either one is entitled to a hinder even though it naturally would be his partner's ball and even though his partner may have attempted to play the ball or that he may already have missed it. It is not a hinder when one player hinders his partner.

4.11 **Avoidable Hinders.** An avoidable hinder results in an "out" or a point depending upon whether the offender was serving or receiving.

(a) **Failure to Move.** Does not move sufficiently to allow opponent his shot.

(b) **Blocking.** Moves into a position effecting a block, on the opponent about to return the ball, or, in doubles, one partner moves in front of an opponent as his partner is returning the ball, or

(c) **Moving into Ball.** Moves in the way and is struck by the ball just played by his opponent.

(d) **Pushing.** Deliberately pushing or shoving an opponent during a volley.

4.12 **Rest Periods.**

(a) **Delays.** Deliberate delay exceeding ten seconds by server, or receiver shall result in an out or point against the offender.

(b) **During Game.** During a game each player in singles, or each side in doubles, either while serving or receiving may request a "time out" for a towel, wiping glasses, change or adjustment. Each "time out" shall not exceed 30 seconds. No more than three "time outs" in a game shall be granted each singles player or each team in doubles.

(c) **Injury.** No time out shall be charged to a player who is injured during play. An injured player shall not be allowed more than a total of fifteen minutes of rest. If the injured player is not able to resume play after total rests of 15 minutes the match shall be awarded to the opponent or opponents. On any further injury to same player, the Commissioner, if present, or committee, after considering any available medical opinion shall determine whether the injured player will be allowed to continue.

(d) A time-out may be called by the referee, at the request of a player and after substantiation by the referee, because of faulty equipment or uniform. Two minutes are to be allowed for any uniform adjustment needed and 30 seconds for any equipment adjustment.

(e) **Between Games.** A two minute rest period is allowed between the first and second games, at which times the players should NOT leave the court, without approval of the referee. A ten minute rest period is allowed between the second and third games, at which time players may leave the court.

(f) **Postponed Games.** Any games postponed by referee due to weather elements shall be resumed with the same score as when postponed.

4.13 **Masters.** Forty will be minimum age for all competition in singles. In doubles, one participant — 40 minimum, the second must be at least 45 years of age.

Part V. Tournaments

5.1 **Draws.**

(a) If possible, the singles draw shall be made at least two days before the tournament commences. The seeding method of drawing shall be approved by the International Racquetball Association.

(b) The draw and seeding committee shall be chaired by the IRA Executive Secretary and shall consist of the Executive Secretary, the National Executive Co-ordinator and the host tournament chairman. No other persons shall participate in the draw or seeding unless at the invitation of the draw and seeding committee.

(c) In local, state and divisional tournaments the draw shall be the responsibility of the tournament chairman. In divisional play the tournament chairman should work in co-ordination with the IRA representative at the tournament.

5.2 **Scheduling.**

(a) **Preliminary Matches.** If one or more contestants are entered in both singles and doubles, they may be required to play both singles and doubles on the same day or night with little rest between matches. This is a risk assumed on entering both singles and doubles. If possible the schedule should provide at least a one hour rest period between all matches.

(b) **Final Matches.** Where one or more players have reached the finals in both singles and doubles, it is recommended that the doubles match be played on the day preceding the singles. This would assume more rest between the final matches. If both final matches must be played on the same day or night, the following procedure is recommended:

(1) The singles match be played first.

(2) A rest period of not less than ONE HOUR be allowed between the finals in singles and doubles.

5.3 **Notice of Matches.** After the first round of matches, it is the responsibility of each player to check the posted schedules to determine the time and place of each subsequent match. If any change is made in the schedule after posting, it shall be the duty of the committee or chairman to notify the players of the change.

5.4 **Third Place.** In championship tournaments; national, state, district, etc., the loser in the semi-finals must play for third place or lose his ranking for the next year unless he is unable to compete because of injury or illness. See Rule 3.5(d)(4).

5.5 **IRA Divisional Tournaments.** Starting in 1969-70 the United States was divided into five divisions.

(a) Only players residing in the area defined can participate in a division tournament.

(b) Players can participate in only two events in a division tournament.

(c) Winners of open singles and open doubles of divisional tournaments will receive round trip air coach tickets to the IRA International Tournament. Renumeration will be made after arrival, entry and play of at least one match.

(1) If the winner(s) of open singles or open doubles has previously won such trip through qualification in a previous IRA-sanctioned tournament, the second place finisher(s) shall be awarded such trip. If the second place finisher(s) also has won such award previously, the third place finisher(s) shall be awarded such trip and so on.

(2) Doubles teams winning divisional championships must remain intact and compete as such in the International Tournament to qualify for this award.

(d) An IRA national officer will be in attendance at each divisional tournament and will coordinate with the host chairman.

Awards:
No individual award in IRA-sanctioned tournaments should exceed value of more than $25.

Tournament Management:
In all IRA-sanctioned tournaments the tournament chairman and/or the national IRA official in attendance may decide on a change of courts after the completion of any tournament game if such a change will accommodate better spectator conditions.

Tournament Conduct:
In all IRA-sanctioned tournaments the referee is empowered to default a match if an individual player or team conducts itself to the detriment of the tournament and the game.

Amateur Definition:
We hold as eligible for racquetball tournaments anyone except those who engage in, or promote racquetball for a profit.

Pick-A-Partner:
The essence of the "Players' Fraternity" has been to allow players to come to tournaments and select a partner, if necessary, regardless what organization or city he might represent.

ONE-WALL AND THREE-WALL RULES

Basically racquetball rules for one-wall, three-wall and four-wall are the same with the following exceptions:

One-Wall

Court Size
Wall shall be 20 ft. in width and 16 ft. high, floor 20 ft. in width and 34 ft. from the wall to the back edge of the long line. There should be a minimum of 3 feet beyond the long line and 6 feet outside each side line and behind the long line to permit movement area for the players.

Short Line
Back edge 16 feet from the wall. Service Markers — Lines at least 6 inches long parallel to and midway between the long and short lines, extending in from the side lines. The imaginary extension and joining of

these lines indicates the service line. Lines are 1½ inches in width. Service Zone — floor area inside and including the short, side and service lines. Receiving Zone — floor area in back of short line bounded by and including the long and side lines.

Three-Wall

Serve

A serve that goes beyond the side walls on the fly is player or side out. A serve that goes beyond the long line on a fly but within the side walls is the same as a "short."

Fundamentals

4

THE GRIP

The grip you use on the paddle or racquet is probably not as important as it is in tennis, since your wrist is used more. Therefore, you may want to experiment with using the eastern forehand and eastern backhand grips or try using the continental grip. The advantage of the continental grip is that it enables you to hit all shots without changing your grip. These different grips are illustrated in Figs. 4.1, 4.2, and 4.3. The eastern forehand is achieved by shaking hands with the paddle or racquet, while the eastern backhand is made by turning your hand one quarter of a turn toward your backhand side. The continental grip is midway between the eastern forehand and backhand.

THE READY POSITION

The position shown in Figure 4.4 is what we will refer to as the ready position. Feet are about shoulder-width apart, knees slightly flexed, weight equally balanced, back fairly straight, head up, and paddle or racquet held out in front of you with elbows bent comfortably. From this position you are now ready to hit from either side as well as move forward or backward to attack or retrieve. It is extremely important that after every shot you try to get back to this position so that you can move to the next shot. The ideal court position for playing is probably mid court and just back of the short line. More will be said later about positions for serving and receiving.

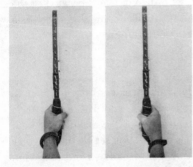

Figure 4.1 (A) Lefthanded forehand grip
(B) Righthanded forehand grip

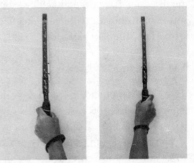

Figure 4.2 (A) Lefthanded backhand grip
(B) Righthanded backhand grip

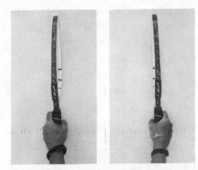

Figure 4.3
(A) Lefthanded continental grip
(B) Righthanded continental grip

Figure 4.4 The ready position

THE BASIC STROKES

The basic strokes in paddle and racquetball are quite similar to those of tennis, so if you have played tennis you will be able to adapt very easily. If you have not played tennis you will be able to master the basic strokes with a little practice. The strokes in paddle and racquetball are much easier to learn and achieve success with than in tennis because of the softer ball, shorter paddle or racquet, and the smaller court size. The basic strokes are the forehand, backhand, volley, and overhead.

The Forehand

The forehand is probably the most important stroke for you to learn and also the easiest. It is important because you will usually serve with a forehand stroke and you will rely on it for the majority of your strong shots. From your ready position, as soon as you see the ball is going to come to your forehand, you must turn your shoulders and take your paddle or racquet back toward the back wall or on a line from the front to the back wall. (See Fig. 4.5.) As you take the paddle or racquet back, make sure you follow the path of the ball with your eyes. You should move your feet so that you are facing the side wall on whichever side of the court the ball is. As you prepare to hit your forehand, your weight should be on the back foot and should be transferred to your forward foot, or "through the shot" as you hit the ball. This is important because the greatest amount of power will come from your weight shift and body rotation, while you use your arm and wrist for control and placement. Your hips and shoulders rotate into the shot to give you even more power. The elbow should be bent at the end of your backswing, and as you stroke through the ball you should let it begin to straighten. The wrist can either remain firm or can be flicked or snapped at the moment of contact. As you hit your forehand you should take a step toward the front wall so that you can have your weight going in that direction.

It is essential that you watch the ball as long as possible, and it will help is you can watch the spot where the ball was contacted for a second after it is actually hit. You can use your forehand anywhere from off your front foot to a position in line with the middle of your body for best results. Do not let the ball get behind you. As you stroke through the ball, let yourself follow through, turn naturally, and then return immediately to your ready position. Fig 4.6 shows the forehand sequence.

Primary Uses
Serving, offense (kill shots, passing shots), defense.

Figure 4.5 Forehand preparation

Figure 4.6 Forehand sequence

The Backhand

The backhand stroke is important for you to master because if you do not, your opponent will beat you on that side. Fortunately the backhand in paddle and racquetball is much easier than in tennis.

As with the forehand, as soon as you see the ball is going to come to your backhand side, you must turn your shoulders and take your paddle or racquet back toward the back wall or on a line from the front to the back wall. (Fig. 4.7.) As you take the paddle or racquet back, make sure that you follow the path of the ball with your eyes and if you are going to use the eastern backhand grip, make this change as you turn your shoulders. As with the forehand, your body should be facing the side wall, weight should be on the rear foot, and transferred to your forward foot or "through the shot" as you hit the ball.

Figure 4.7 Backhand preparation

The arm and wrist position differ from that of the forehand in that you should keep both straight as you hit the shot. Bending or breaking the elbow at contact is not as crucial a mistake as it is in tennis, but it will cause a loss of power and accuracy. The wrist can either remain firm at contact or can be flicked or snapped to redirect the ball. However, flicking or snapping takes excellent timing and should be considered a more advanced skill. You should take a step toward the front wall as you hit the backhand and let your hips and shoulders turn naturally through the shot.

Remember, watch the spot where the ball was contacted for a second after the hit to ensure solid contact and maximum accuracy. You should try to hit your backhand anywhere from off your forward foot to a position in line with the middle of your body. Do not let the ball get behind you, and as soon as you hit, feel as though you are pulling through from your shoulder into the ball. Fig. 4.8 illustrates the backhand sequence.

Figure 4.8 Backhand sequence

You should think of developing your backhand at first as a defensive weapon so that every time the ball is hit to your backhand you can return it without giving your opponent the opportunity to win the point. If you give your backhand a chance, it can become your most consistent stroke, and as you gain confidence in it you can start to develop it as an offensive weapon as well. Remember, after you hit the shot, return quickly to the ready position so you are prepared for the next shot.

Primary Uses
Offense (kill shots, passing shots), defense.

The Volley

A volley is a ball that you will hit before it has a chance to bounce on the floor of the court. In order to hit this shot you must do three essential things. The volleyed ball must be watched closely and you must step into the shot while keeping the wrist very firm.

The simplest method of volleying involves very little or no backswing and therefore it is important to step into the ball in order to obtain power. By keeping the wrist firm through the shot, greater accuracy and control is gained. This is where the continental grip is superior, because it eliminates the need to change your grip for forehand and backhand shots. When hitting the volley you should try to step with your opposite foot on the forehand and the same foot on the backhand. For example, if you are right handed step forward with your left foot for your forehand volleys, and your right foot for your backhand volleys. (Fig. 4.9 and 4.10) As you hit your forehand volley, think of pushing your wrist away from your body, and on your backhand volley think of pushing your elbow away. This will help in squaring up the face of your paddle or racquet ot your target. (Fig. 4.11 and 4.12.)

Primary Uses

Offense (kill shots, dink shots, passing shots, fly kills and passes, offensive lobs), defense.

Figure 4.9 The forehand volley step   **Figure 4.10** The backhand volley step

Figure 4.11 Wrist away on the forehand volley

Figure 4.12 The elbow away on the backhand volley

The Overhead

This shot should be an easy one because it is essentially the same motion as you use in the tennis serve, throwing a baseball, or spiking a volleyball. The major difference is that there is not as much downward wrist snap because you should use this shot mainly for lobbing, passing, and sometimes serving.

To hit this shot, try to turn sideways to the ball so you can rotate your hips and shoulders into the shot, and as you hit the ball let your weight shift from your back foot to your front foot. You should take the paddle or racquet back behind your head and your elbow should point towards the ceiling. (Fig. 4.13) As you hit the ball, letting your weight shift and body rotate, extend your elbow into the ball and at contact use your wrist to direct the ball.

This shot can be hit easily from a lazy position of facing the front wall, but often the result is a ball hit down into the floor. Try to get into the proper position and watch the spot after contact. Contact the ball at a point just below the extent of your reach and just out in front of you. Fig. 4.14 illustrates this shot.

Primary Uses
Offense (passing, lobbing), defense (lobbing, ceiling shot).

Figure 4.13 The racquet down the back for the overhead and ceiling shot

Figure 4.14 Overhead sequence

FOOTWORK

We mentioned briefly the importance of good footwork. This is really the foundations to a good game in paddle or racquetball as it is in handball, tennis, or squash racquets. Rarely will the ball be hit so that it comes to you in perfect position for your return. You must train yourself to react quickly and move as soon as the ball leaves the front wall (or before if possible). Remember, as you move, take your paddle or racquet back as you go for the shot so that you can make the stroke when you arrive at the right spot. Try to be facing the wall on the side the shot will be taken and position yourself so that you can step toward the front wall on the shot to give yourself the added power of your weight shift, and to enable your hips and shoulders to rotate into the shot.

One of the most difficult parts of the game, which you will have to work on, is determining the correct distance away from the ball, so that you can make the desired shot. Do not get discouraged as practice will soon help you improve. Try, when you are on the court, never to be caught standing still while the ball is in play — always be moving. This will help insure that you have a chance to be in position for every shot.

WHEN TO STROKE

Stroking the ball is extremely important from both a psychological and strategic standpoint. Practice will enable you to become proficient at stroking as well as hitting the ball. The ball must be hit at one of three points; in the air, just after it bounces, or after it bounces and starts its downward arc. The volleyed ball, hit on the fly before it bounces, is often a difficult shot because of speed, angle and body position. A ball hit just after it bounces, or half-volleyed, is an even more difficult shot and will be discussed later on. The ideal ball position is after it has bounced and is on its downward arc. The ball will have slowed down, you will have had more time to get into position and to watch the ball, and the lower the ball is contacted the better your chances are to kill the shot. Of course you are not always going to be able to hit the ball from this ideal position and therefore should practice hitting the ball from all three positions. Fig. 4.15 illustrates these positions.

BEGINNING THE SKILLS

If you have never played handball, paddleball, racquetball, or squash racquets before, one of the biggest adjustments you will have to make is

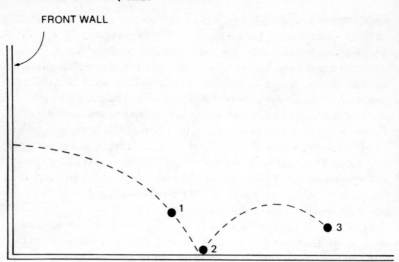

Figure 4.15 Three places to contact the ball: (1) volley or fly, (2) half-volley, (3) ideal position for beginners

getting accustomed to the court. Most people are used to playing in a wide open or semienclosed space, and moving into a small enclosed room takes some adjustment. As you walk into the court for the first time, take a look around and try to imagine the many different bounces that a ball can take off of the four walls, floor, and ceiling. As you become acquainted with your court, go to the back and stand a couple of feet from the back wall in the center and face the front wall. Now close your eyes and point to a particular spot on the front or side wall. Open your eyes and see how close you are to being on that point. You will probably be surprised to find yourself pretty close, if not right on the spot. The reason for having you do this is simple: if you can close your eyes and mentally picture every spot in the court, you will be able to concentrate on watching the ball during play. Further, since a great majority of shots are missed because they are not watched closely enough, you will be able to eliminate many of these. This is a skill you should practice for a few seconds or longer every time you walk into the court.

The next assignment for you when you come into the court is to stand in the back court and practice just throwing the ball at the front wall. Warm up slowly so that your arm and shoulder do not become sore. (This should be done as a warmup prior to every workout.) As you throw the ball, observe the way it reacts and the way it bounces. Next throw the ball so that it rebounds off the side and back walls and then the front wall and again observe how the ball bounces. Throw some at the ceiling and watch to see if they reach the front wall, and if they do, how they bounce and at what angles.

Once you have acquainted yourself with how the ball bounces, you are then ready to move for the ball. Repeat the throwing drills, and this time try to move and position yourself so that you can catch the ball in the air in position to either hit the ball in the air (volley), or on the first bounce. Practice this off the back wall and around the back corners, as these will be vary common shots.

After you have done this and find out that you are starting to move fairly well with the ball, try to hit a few (easy) shots with your hand; palm for forehand and back of your hand for backhand. Do not try to hit the ball hard, as the purpose of this drill is merely to get you into position to hit the shots.

You are now ready to take your paddle or racquet into the court with you. Make sure that the thong is secure around your wrist so that if your grip slips you will not lose the paddle or racquet. Assume your back court position and after your warmup procedures, face your forehand wall, bounce the ball and stroke the forehand to the front wall. Repeat this until you feel the shot coming very smoothly and effortlessly. Now face the backhand wall and repeat the same drill. Remember to watch the spot where contact was made for a second after the ball has been hit. Feel your weight shift as you step into the shot and try to be aware of the power that your hips and shoulders lend to the shot as they rotate into the contact area. Make your follow-through natural and easy and experiment with keeping the wrist firm versus snapping it as you contact the ball. Try to determine which method gives more accuracy, which more power, and which is the more consistent method. Which do you prefer?

Now proceed to the drill of hitting off the back wall and around the corners. This drill is important since you will have many of these shots during a game and they are more difficult than shots straight off the front or back wall. Stand about eight feet from the back wall, hit a strong forehand or backhand to the front wall so that it will rebound off the back wall, and practice moving, stepping with, and hitting both forehands and backhands back to the front wall. (Fig. 4.16) Hit some so that they are returned to a side wall and then the front wall. Now practice following the ball around the back corners. Be patient and give yourself enough room to swing. Try to step with the shot to give yourself adequate power. (Fig. 4.17.)

This shot is much more difficult than the ball that comes straight off the back wall so you should spend extra time on this drill. There is

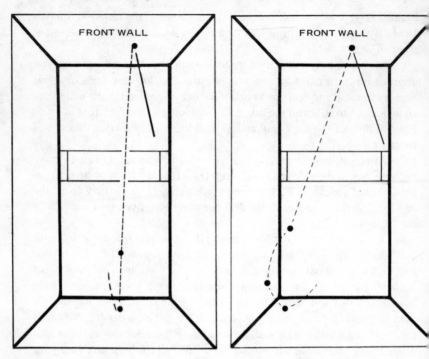

Figure 4.16 Ball coming directly off rear wall

Figure 4.17 Ball coming around left rear corner

really no substitute for practice, so try to devote some time each session to this shot, both backhand and forehand, as well as the other shots.

Once you have come this far with your drills and skill progressions, you are ready to begin working with a partner. You or your partner start serving (see Chapter 5) and the other receiving. Do not play more than the return of serve, each of you serve ten to twenty serves, and then rotate. In this manner you will each get to practice both serving and returning.

Following this drill you will be eager to play a game (if you have not attempted to already), so go ahead. However, remember that at the beginning the score is not as important as moving, watching the ball, court position, and strokes. From the very start, try to set up a game plan in your mind: think about the ideal position to be in, what your opponent's strengths and weaknesses are, and what your own are, and utilize this knowledge while playing. Make mental notes on your weaknesses so that you can practice them later. Review the stroke fundamentals and the rules (Chapter 3), so that you are familiar with them. While you are learning to play do not be afraid to stop and discuss with your partner or teacher any questions pertaining to rules, etc. This is how you learn. Remember, the objectives of paddle or racquetball are exercise and enjoyment. Certainly you enjoy winning, but unless you become an accomplished tournament player, this should not be your main goal. You will probably learn more from losing than you will from winning so let every match or practice session be a learning experience.

TRAINING HINTS

A paddle or racquetball player can become a better player by being in good physical shape. In a match between two players of equal ability, the one who is more fit will usually win. You can benefit greatly by performing a regular workout which may include the exercises listed below. You may not want to bother with them at all, so just a few or you may want to really work out. Whichever you choose to do, remember to start out slowly and build up gradually. Extra work always pays off.

Exercise	Purpose
Pushups	Arm and shoulder strength
Situps	Abdominal strength
Jumping rope	Footwork and leg strength
Squeezing an old tennis ball	Grip and forearm strength
Distance running	Endurance
Short sprints	Speed
Staring at a paddle or racquetball	Concentration

The
Serve

5

The serve is simply the method of putting the ball into play. Its importance in the games of racquetball and paddleball cannot be overlooked. A good serve permits the server to remain on offense and in control of the game. A poorly served ball often results in the receiver gaining control of the point and possibly the game. How you should serve to an opponent is determined by your particular strengths and his evident weaknesses. Never serve just to put the ball into play; have a plan and try to implement it. By varying the height, direction and speed of your serve, you will keep your opponent off-balance and thus help keep yourself on the offense.

How you hit your serve is dependent upon what you do with your racquet or paddle. The angle of the racquet or paddle face, the wrist action, and the point at which the ball is struck, all influence the direction, speed and height of the serve as it is delivered.

There are four basic serves which should be mastered by all players regardless of playing level. Take your time, however, and make sure you become fairly competent at one or two before trying to master all. These are the power or drive serve, the lob serve, the cross court serve, and the overhead serve. Remember that the best serve to use is one that will travel toward your opponent's weaker side. In most cases, this will be his backhand. By varying your serve in terms of height, speed, and direction you can help to avoid a repetitious type of delivery and this will keep your opponent from becoming too familiar with your service pattern. Mastery of the serve will add greatly to your success in either paddleball or racquetball and will keep the games challenging as your level of skill increases.

When delivering the serve, the basic forehand stroking position is the most desirable. Begin by facing the front wall, take your forehand backswing and pivot so that the hip opposite your swing is parallel to the front wall. For example, if you are righthanded you would pivot to your right and your left hip would then be parallel to the front wall. Figs. 5.1 and 5.2 illustrate these positions. Lefthanded servers will find their right hip parallel to the front wall, as they will pivot to their left. Be sure to step across in the pivot with your lead foot. This insures a good base of support when you swing forward to meet the ball.

Figure 5.1 Ready position for the serve   **Figure 5.2** Preparation for the serve

Sometimes it is best to predetermine which type of serve you will hit. However, many times this will depend on the position of your opponent, which serves he has difficulty returning, and your mental attitude at that time. Once the ball has left the racquet or paddle face its direction has been determined. Your accuracy is determined by the angle of the racquet or paddle at contact with the ball, while speed must come from the backswing, contact, and follow-through.

THE POWER SERVE

Let us assume that you choose to deliver a power serve. Hold the ball in the hand opposite your racquet or paddle hand. Flex your knees and bend at the waist, take your pivot step and backswing. Then, drop the ball so that it will rebound to about waist height, and far enough in front of you so that the swing will be into the ball and permit the easy, long follow-through necessary for an effective and powerful delivery. Hit the serve after the ball has reached the top of its bounce, has started to drop and is somewhere around knee height. As you hit this serve make sure to keep your eyes on the ball and stride into the shot for extra power. Try to imagine where you want the ball to contact the front wall and then where it will go. Fig. 5.3 illustrates the power or drive serve.

Figure 5.3 Power serve sequence

The ball should rebound off the front wall and land as close to the rear corner of the court as possible. This is best accomplished by having the ball strike the lower one-third of the front wall. If you attempt to hit the serve from a higher position it will usually rebound too high off the front wall and result in an easy return for your opponent. Figure 5.4 shows this pathway. The optional placement of the power serve is achieved by hitting the ball low on the front wall so that it hits the floor as close behind the short line as possible. This will cause the receiver to move forward and possibly be off balance while attempting his return. (Fig. 5.4)

Regardless of which form of the power serve you use, effectiveness is gained from the force with which it is delivered.

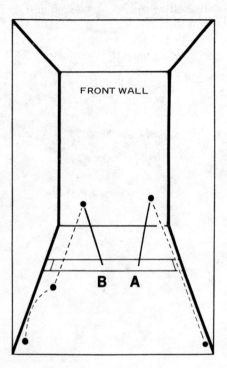

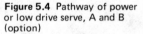
Figure 5.4 Pathway of power or low drive serve, A and B (option)

THE LOB SERVE

A second serve you should learn is the lob. It should be delivered with less force than the power serve, in an effort to obtain good control and placement of the ball as it leaves the racquet or paddle face. The footwork, pivot, ball release and body posture are similar to those of the power serve, except that you should open your stance toward the front wall when executing this shot. Fig 5.5 illustrates the lob serve.

Court position is important, and for a lob serve to be effective, it should be delivered from a position close to the side wall along which the ball is to be served. The serve is made by striking the ball on an upward arc so that it hits about three-quarters of the way up the front wall. It

Figure 5.5 Lob serve sequence

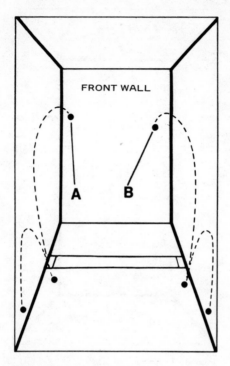

Figure 5.6 Pathway of lob serve,
A and B (option)

should then rebound in a long, slow arc, landing in the rear of the court on the side it was served. (Fig. 5.6A.)

You can also use an optional placement of the lob serve, in a deceptive effort, by standing in midcourt as though you were going to execute a power serve. The delivery, however, should be easy as the racquet or paddle is brought into the ball. Too slow a backswing may "telegraph" your intentions, so try not to be too obvious. When the ball is served from this midcourt position it should be angled off the front wall and into the rear corners. (Fig. 5.6B.)

As with the power serve, the lob serve hit so that it is awkward for your opponent will increase the difficulty of its return. The soft, slow, dropping ball offers a somewhat easy target to hit if it is not as close to the wall as possible. Keeping the ball close to the side wall will often result in either a missed return or one which is high to the middle of the front wall. The latter will rebound directly back to the server, and he will be in an excellent position to win the point.

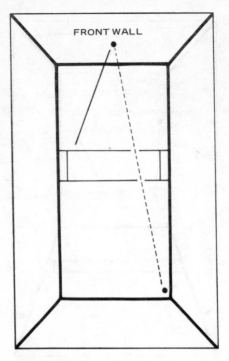

FRONT WALL

Figure 5.7 Pathway of cross court serve

THE CROSS COURT SERVE

Once you have mastered the power serve and the lob serve, you should be ready for the cross court serve. This serve, like the lob, has two variations: the direct cross court and the high cross court delivery or "z" serve. The first of these, the direct cross court serve, should be easy for you to master. It is considered one of the easiest serves to deliver and can be quite effective. To make it effective, take a position to the side of the court as if you were going to hit a lob serve directly down the side wall. As you take your basic forehand stroke to deliver the serve, strike the ball so that it hits the center of the front wall. A ball hit in such a manner should rebound deep to the opposite corner of the court (Fig. 5.7.)

Further effectiveness and variety can be attained with the high cross court or "z" serve. Take the same position as you did when hitting the cross court serve, and strike the ball so that it hits about three-quarters of the way up the front wall near the corner opposite your serving position. A good, strong follow-through is essential to produce enough force to insure the effectiveness of this serve. The ball should strike the front wall near the corner, angle to the side wall, and then carry about two-thirds of the length of the court before hitting the floor. After hitting the floor the ball should still have enough momentum to bounce toward the opposite side wall or the back wall. Fig. 5.8 illustrates this.

In order to return either the cross court or the "z" serve effectively, the receiver must be extremely alert to the movement of the ball. Because of the speed at which the ball is moving, the receiver must meet the ball accurately or his return shot will be very weak or missed entirely. The "z" and cross court serves may force the receiver to "dig" his shot out of the corner, very often resulting in a weak return and therefore an easy point for the server.

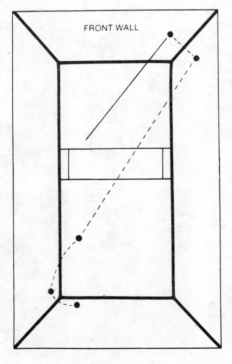

FRONT WALL

Figure 5.8 Pathway of "z" serve

THE OVERHEAD SERVE

Lob serves and cross court serves can also be hit from the overhead position. To execute these from this position, assume your normal stance, bounce the ball high in the air and hit whichever shot you desire. The lob serve will be hit softly and the cross court serve will be hit hard. The height at which the ball is contacted should be almost as high as you can comfortably reach with your racquet or paddle, and the ball should be about six to eight inches in front of you. Practice the bounce because it is higher than for the other serves and requires more control. This method of serving is more advanced and requires better timing and more accuracy. Its real value lies in deception, and it offers you another method of putting the ball in play. Fig. 5.9 illustrates the overhead serve.

Figure 5.9 Overhead serve sequence

The Basic Shots

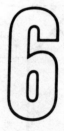

The basic shots in paddle and racquetball are almost identical to those of handball, with the addition of the lob. As a review (or if you have never played handball), the shots are pass, kill, lob, ceiling, and wall. The basic shots can be broken down into two categories: offensive and defensive. The kills and passing shots are offensive shots while the ceiling, lob and three-wall shots are basically defensive. You should set a goal of trying to become as competent as possible with all of these shots. As you begin to play, you will find that most of the points are won on mistakes rather than good shots. The more proficient you become, though, the more points you will have to win outright on good shots (i.e., pass or kill).

OFFENSE

In order to be a steady, consistent player you must strive to become an offensive player and not rely on defense alone. Unlike tennis, it is very difficult ot be a back court player in either paddle or racquetball. Let's start with the shots.

The Passing Shot

This shot will probably be the easiest for you to master and you will have more immediate success with it. The offensive pass is generally made from the front court and the defensive pass from the back court. The basic idea of the passing shot is to stroke the ball hard and out of reach of your opponent so that a return is not possible. Perhaps the best position for you to make this shot from is when your opponent is in the front court and you are behind him, or he is on the far side or a rear corner of the court. Try to keep your passing shot wide ot the outside of the court and try to hit it so that it dies at the back wall. There are two types of passing shots: the straight pass and the two-wall pass. The straight pass (Fig. 6.1) hits the front wall directly and rebounds toward the backwall without touching the side wall. The two-wall pass (Fig. 6.2) hits the front wall directly, then hits the side wall just behind the short line about two feet above the floor, and then proceeds to the back court.

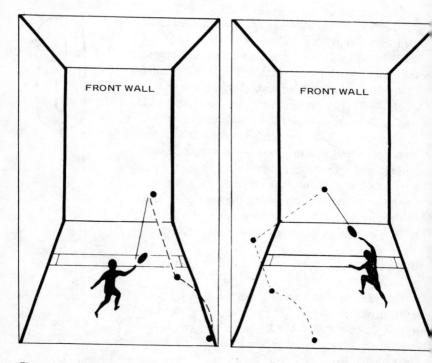

Figure 6.1 The straight pass shot

Figure 6.2 The two-wall pass shot

The passing shot can be effective as a defensive weapon as well when you are off balance and your opponent is out of position. Remember that to be effective, the passing shot must hit the front wall first, be struck with sufficient force so that your opponent does not have time to reach it, and must be hit wide and not too high. The passing shot can be made with either the forehand, backhand, overhead or volley stroke. The fly pass is simply a passing shot hit before it has a chance to bounce on the floor or side wall. This shot can be volleyed or hit overhead and is probably most effectively executed from the front court position. Remember to watch the ball very closely and try not to take the ball too high in the air.

The Kill Shot

The kill shot in paddle and racquetball is undoubtedly the most devastating offensive weapon you can develop. When hit correctly it offers little or no chance of a return, and aside from winning points outright, this can demoralize your opponent. The kill shot is a must if you desire to become a good player. The shot is one that hits the front wall very close to the floor in such a manner that it does not rebound up, but comes almost straight out only a few inches from the floor. There are two basic kill shots: the straight kill and the corner kill. The straight kill (Fig. 6.3)

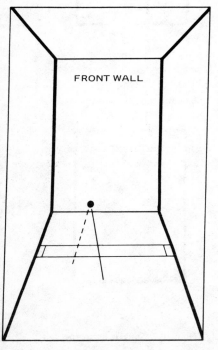

FRONT WALL

Figure 6.3 Straight kill

hits the front wall directly and rebounds toward the back wall without touching a side wall.

The corner kill can be one of four types (listed below) and it hits the front and side wall before coming out. The most effective kill shots are those that are kept close to the side walls. The corner kills are: inside right corner, which hits the front wall first and then the right wall (Fig. 6.4); outside right corner, which hits the right wall first and then the front wall (Fig. 6.5); inside left corner kill, which hits the front wall first and then the left wall (Fig. 6.6); and outside left corner, which hits the left wall first and then the front wall (Fig. 6.7).

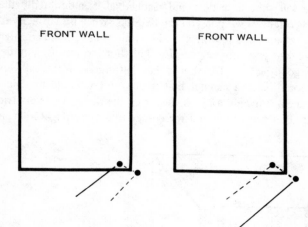

Figure 6.4 Inside right corner kill   **Figure 6.5** Outside right corner kill

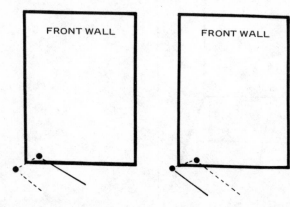

Figure 6.6 Inside left corner kill   **Figure 6.7** Outside left corner kill

In order to become proficient at hitting kill shots you must practice them, and some important points to keep in mind are:

1. Let the ball drop low, knee height or lower.
2. Keep your eye on the ball.
3. Step into the shot with knees bent.
4. Keep your racquet arm parallel to the floor.
5. Follow through toward the intended direction of the shot.

Figs. 6.8 and 6.9 illustrate the forehand and backhand kill shots.

Figure 6.8 Forehand kill sequence

Figure 6.9 Backhand kill sequence

Kill shots should be practiced from all parts of the court. Remember, in order to hit an effective kill shot you must be in good position and have good balance, otherwise you will probably only set your opponent up for a good shot. You can execute the kill shots with the forehand, backhand and volley strokes.

The fly kill is hit before it can bounce and like the fly pass it requires greater timing and concentration. This shot is probably best executed from the front court with the volley stroke. Remember to let the ball drop as low as you can, bend over, and follow through low. Try to hit a couple of kill shots from too high a position. You will find that the ball bounces up and may set up your opponent, so stay down. A good rule to follow when hitting your kill shots is to aim about six inches off the floor; that way if you make an error you will still have a chance of making a good shot.

DEFENSE

In order to become a good paddle or racquetball player you must be able to combine defense with offense. The reason for this is simply that you will not always be on the offense or in position for an offensive shot. If you can hit good defensive shots you can save yourself many points and win many more matches. Remember, a defensive shot is not designed to win a point outright, but merely to get you into an offensive position.

The three basic defensive shots are the ceiling shot, the lob and the three-wall shot.

The Ceiling Shot

This shot is made from the back court when your opponent is in front of you. Generally the shot is hit with the overhead stroke and occasionally with either the forehand or backhand stroke. The most important aspect of the ceiling shot is where it contacts the ceiling. The ball should be struck so that it hits the ceiling anywhere from one to five feet in front of the front wall, then strikes the front wall, rebounds high off the floor in the front court, and continues into the back court, where ideally it should hit low on the back wall before striking the floor. Fig. 6.10 illustrates the ceiling shot. If the ball strikes the ceiling too far from the front wall it may never reach it, and if the shot is hit too hard the ball may rebound too far off the back wall and give your opponent a setup. Practice is essential to obtain a feel as to how hard to hit this shot.

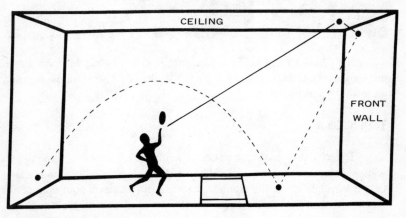

CEILING

FRONT WALL

Figure 6.10 The ceiling shot

The overhead ceiling shot is struck out in front of the forehead, should be stepped into, and the paddle or racquet should follow through toward the target. The amount of wrist used in this shot will depend on your position in the court, your strength, and the speed of the ball being contacted. Remember that the hitting shoulder should be lower than the lead shoulder for best results. Fig. 6.11 shows the execution of the overhead ceiling shot.

Figure 6.11
Overhead ceiling sequence

The forehand and backhand ceiling shots are usually hit from above the waist and the only difference in the stroke is a higher follow through up toward the ceiling.

The Lob Shot

The lob can be a offensive shot as well as a defensive one, though you will probably use it more as a defensive shot. The defensive lob is a shot that is hit high up on the front wall so that it just clears your opponent's reach and then dies in the back court. The ideal time to hit this shot is when your opponent is in the front court and you are behind him, but perhaps not in a good position or balance to attempt a kill or passing shot. If your opponent is in the back court you cannot lob over him. The lob can be straight (Fig. 6.12), in which there is no rebound off a side wall, or it can be a two-wall lob (Fig. 6.13), in which the ball, after hitting the front wall, hits the side wall about five feet from the back wall, dies and goes straight up the back wall.

The strung racquet has the advantage over the paddle for the lob shot because more underspin can be put on the ball and the shot will lose its speed much more rapidly.

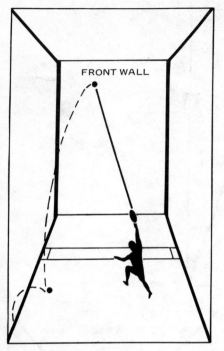

FRONT WALL

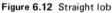

Figure 6.12 Straight lob

The Three-Wall Shot

This shot can be an effective defensive weapon when you are caught in the back court. The properly executed shot strikes three walls before hitting the floor, which should give you ample time to get into an offensive position. The secret to this shot is to hit it hard and position it so that it strikes the first side wall about 15 feet above the floor and so that it will rebound off the front wall close to the opposite side wall and at about the same height. If this shot is hit correctly it will then land about eight feet behind the short line and rebound off the side wall about four feet from the back wall. Fig. 6.14 shows this rebounding action.

The shot is very similar to the "z" serve explained in Chapter 5, page 58. You must experiment with this shot to really know what it will do. If you hit it too softly you will set your opponent up for an easy shot. If you hit the front wall too near the center, the ball will probably rebound off the back wall and again set up your opponent. You should also experiment with different amounts and types of spins to see what results they will give you. To make the three-wall shot you can use either the forehand,

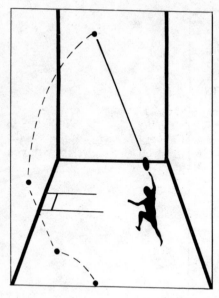

Figure 6.13 Two-wall lob

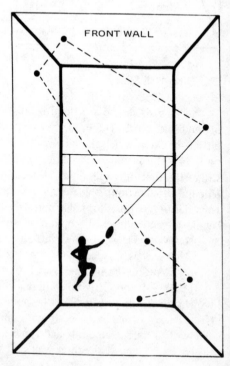

FRONT WALL

Figure 6.14 Three-wall shot

backhand (if it is strong enough), or overhead stroke. Remember to step into the shot and follow through in the direction of the target. Experiment with different heights, speeds, and contact points from different court positions.

PRACTICING THE BASIC SHOTS

The old saying that "practice makes perfect" is very appropriate in the games of paddle and racquetball. The more times you can practice the basic shots, the more proficient you will become. However, before you tackle the shots, go back and review the basic strokes, footwork, and warm up. Take your paddle or racquet and ball or ask your coach for a bucket of old balls and go into a court by yourself. Position yourself in the front court, face one wall or the other, bounce a ball, let it drop to knee height or lower, and practice your straight kill shot. Then proceed to the various corner kills and as you become fairly proficient from the front court begin to move back until you are finally at the back wall. Try this method with all of the shots (the lob and the three-wall shots do not need to be practiced from the front court, though you may want to try them from that position), and concentrate on hitting the shots with all the different strokes. Remember, you cannot become a complete player if you cannot hit a respectable backhand or one of the other strokes. Practice the shots while concentrating on good stroke mechanics and be patient; remember that it takes time to develop both strokes and shots.

Once you start to become adept at some of the shots, begin to practice a sequence of shots. For example, stand just behind the short line and hit a lob or ceiling shot over your head and then go back and try to retrieve it. This type of combination can work with many shots. Do not be afraid to experiment. Next, work with a partner. One of you practice passing shots while the other tries to retrieve them and gain the offensive position. Again, many such combinations can be worked out. Now, with lots of practice and playing, you are ready to begin work on some strategy. You can no longer just walk into the court and begin banging the ball aimlessly around. Every game must have a plan.

The Game
of
Singles

7

In all of sport there is nothing quite like the game of singles, whether it be tennis, handball, squash, paddle or racquetball. You are on your own and are responsible for your own good and bad shots. Success or failure lies solely on your own performance. However, the two main objectives of the game are exercise and enjoyment. Everyone prefers to win, but remember the old adage: for every winner there must be a loser. If the right attitude is taken, though, losing can and should only involve a point total and final score. Everyone who plays the game should win from the standpoint of exercise, pleasure, the thrill of making some great shots, and a feeling of sportsmanship. It is just as important to be a good loser as it is a good winner.

THE SERVER

This is the most important man in the game. He is on the offense and he alone has the power, through his serve, to determine how the game will proceed. Therefore it is vital for you to develop the most effective serves that you can. Review Chapter 5 and practice hard. You must be able to use a variety of serves to enable you to overcome the strengths of your opponent, to change the pace of the game, and to remain on the offense and in control of the game. The serve is the only phase of the game where one of you has control over the ball. Therefore take your time and watch the ball closely. As you step into the service box have a game plan in mind. Hit to your opponent's weakness(es) and try to imagine where his return will come so that you can be ready for it. Always try to think a couple of shots ahead. You may have to alter this plan according to your opponent's return, but experiment with the idea. As the server, you occupy the front court and from this position hold a great advantage. Try to keep this advantage by not letting your opponent out of the back court. Search for his weaknesses. How does he handle lob serves to his backhand? Does he run around his backhand on the "z" serve to that side? Be creative as you serve and play, *do not just put the ball in play*. Every person you play with is going to have different strengths and weaknesses and this can strengthen your game. Do not play with the same person all the time as your game can become very stereo-typed. Learn to feel out your different opponents for their particular strengths and weaknesses.

Just as in tennis, there are three important factors that make up a good serve. Placement (control), spin, and depth are far more important at the beginning than power. After you have developed these three factors you can start to concentrate on hitting the ball harder on the serve and developing a good power serve. Remember, you should strive to accomplish three things for a good offensive serve:
1. Hit to your opponent's weakness(es).
2. Keep the ball from rebounding too strongly off the back wall, thus setting your opponent up.
3. Hit the serve close to the side walls and deep into the rear corners; make your opponent really have to dig to get the serve back.

RETURN OF SERVE

When you are in the position of returning the serve, you must have one goal in mind. Do not let the server win a point without having to hit the ball a second time. Take up a position in the center of the court and a couple of steps away from the back wall. As the server prepares to serve, watch him carefully, notice how he stands, which direction he faces, and how he takes the paddle or racquet back to stroke the ball. Just prior to his hitting the serve take a small hop or jump step to get yourself moving for the return. Watch how he strikes the ball and then concentrate solely on the flight of the ball. Try to determine as quickly as possible what type of serve has been hit, where you are going to have to be to return it and what type of return you can use.

As the serve is contacted, begin taking your paddle or racquet back for your return and start moving into position to hit your return. The serve will either be an effective shot or an ineffective one. If the serve is poorly hit and you can obtain a good position and good balance to hit an offensive return, do so. However, if the serve is hard to handle, your main objective is to return the best you can; ideally with a good defensive shot that will move the server out of the front court and give you a chance to move into it. As you play and practice more you will become more adept at returning the serve effectively so as not to set your opponent up for an easy point.

Remember to watch the ball through the hit of the return and follow through in the direction of your shot. When moving to make the return do not position yourself too close ot the spot of contact, but stop a step or two away so that you can stride into the return. When you must return a lob serve or a high cross court or "z" serve that drops too low, it very often is a good idea to hit a fly shot. This can accomplish two things: it may catch your opponent off balance and it will save you from having to go to the back wall for your return. Remember though that the fly shot requires good timing and balance and you cannot be late in hitting it. Practice returning the serve with all of your strokes and practice all of the shots. The stronger your return of serve (either offensive or defensive) becomes, the better player you will become. Three points to remember in returning the serve are: take the offensive advantage away from the server, generally play a safe shot, and watch your opponent for any hints he may give away.

PLAYING STRATEGY

A successful game in any sport must have a plan of some sort lest the game turn into a mere struggle and scramble. Before starting your match try to develop a game plan or strategy to follow as the game progresses. Granted, the plan may have to be altered at times but without a plan it is very difficult to attack and you will find yourself merely reacting to your opponent's shots.

As the server, plan your serve and the shot that will most likely follow, based on the probable returns your opponent may come up with. As the receiver, plan your return (attack or defense), and the next probable shot and court position. Analyze your opponent's strengths and weaknesses. If he is strong, but lacks stamina or speed, plan on running him and try to tire him. Use a variety of passing shots, lobs, etc. If your opponent has a very weak backhand, hit the majority of shots to that side, and when he starts to protect the weak side, exploit the other side. If you lack endurance and stamina you will have to move in quickly and try for fast points — kills, fly shots, etc. If a particular shot or series of shots (from serve to kill to three-wall) is working well for you, do not change it until your opponent begins to have success in handling the shots. Game strategy consists of both offense and defense, and it is important that you strive to develop both of these aspects of the game.

OFFENSE

Your offensive strategy is probably the most important, because offense is generally what wins points and games. The most important offensive shot in paddle and racquetball is the kill shot. You can never become a good player if you do not develop this shot. The kill shot should be practiced from all areas of the court and practiced with forehand, backhand and volley strokes. This is a must. Therefore, practice, practice, practice!

When you are in the front court and your opponent is behind you, the corner kills are good shots. Hit them so that the ball goes away from your opponent and generally toward his weak side. Figs. 7.1 through 7.4 illustrate this.

When your opponent is to one side of you or in front of you, the straight kill down a side wall is a good shot, and again aim preferably for his weak side. (Fig. 7.5.)

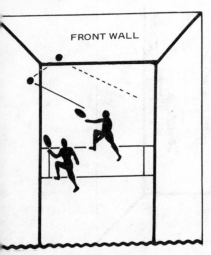
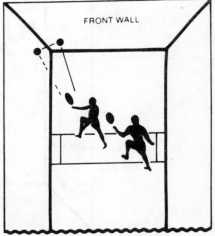

Figure 7.1 Outside left corner kill

Figure 7.2 Inside left corner kill

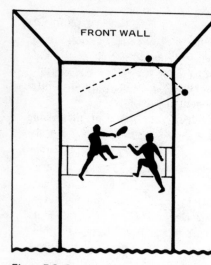

Figure 7.3 Outside right corner kill

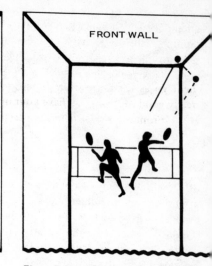

Figure 7.4 Inside right corner kill

Figure 7.5 The straight kill shot

When hitting your offensive shots, try to position yourself so that you will be between your opponent and where the ball will end up (review Rules, Chapter 3, on hinders), and generally try to hit the shot to his weak side. When planning your shots, do so with the idea of making your opponent go as far as possible to return the shot. Then if you do not hit a really good shot you still have your opponent at a disadvantage.

From a position behind or to the side of your opponent, the passing shot (straight or two-wall) is an excellent shot. (Fig. 7.6 and 7.7.) Make sure that you hit your passing shots hard enough and close enough to the side walls so that your opponent cannot cut them off, but must retreat to the backcourt to retrieve them.

The subject of fly kills and fly passes is too often overlooked and neglected. These shots are like the poach in tennis doubles: unexpected, very quick, and usually very effective. Any time you have a chance to hit one of these shots and are in good position and balance to do so, attempt one. Most of the time you will catch your opponent off balance, and even if you do not hit the shot perfectly you will have a good chance of winning

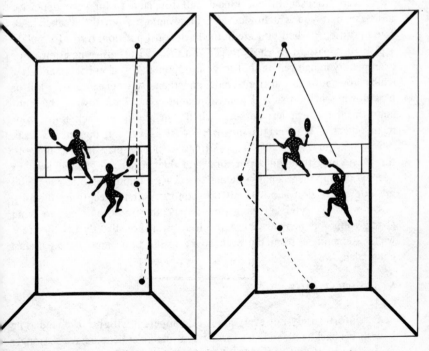

Figure 7.6 The straight pass shot

Figure 7.7 The two-wall pass shot

the point because your opponent will not be prepared. However, it is important that you practice these shots because they do require a great deal of timing and concentration. Try to apply the same principles to the strategy of these shots as was discussed above.

DEFENSE

As stated previously, to be a complete paddle or racquetball player, you must have a good defense as well as an offense. Anytime you are put in a position where you cannot execute one of the offensive shots, you must be able to make a good defensive shot if you are to remain in the game. Therefore, it is essential that you work to develop a good ceiling shot, lob, and three-wall shot. Remember that these shots will almost always be used from the back court, though on occasion you may want to lob volley from the front court if you are caught off balance and your opponent is moving to the front court. Experiment with putting under-spin on or slicing the ball and you will find that you can drop the ball very neatly in the back corners. See Fig. 6.12, page 69.

Learn to use both backhand and forehand to hit your defensive shots, so that you will not be at a disadvantage from the weaker back court position. When you are in the back court position, try to formulate a plan or a pattern of shots to get you into the offensive position. For example, try a high ceiling shot to your opponent's weaker backhand, after which you move to the front court, and then try to execute a fly kill or pass down the right side as your opponent comes back toward the front court from the rear left corner. When you are in the back court, your main objective is to get to the front court. Play your opponent's weak side, watch for an opening for an offensive shot; or play defense, move to the front court following your shot, and then either put the ball away or keep your opponent on the defensive. A very important rule when you hit a defensive shot is not to hit the front wall first (exception: the lob), in order to give yourself more time to gain the front court and to avoid giving your opponent a chance to intercept a shot directly off the front wall. Remember, from the back court position you must have patience and a plan.

YOUR WEAK SIDE

Unfortunately not everyone is as competent with his forehand as he is with his backhand, and vice versa. As a rule most people have a stronger forehand than backhand. Therefore, it is vitally important that you work hard to develop your weak side. If you do not, you are leaving yourself open for many shots to that side, and you will make many more mistakes. You may never become equally proficient from both sides and this is not a great problem, for you can take many shots with your stronger side. Any ball that you can reasonably step around for a strong side shot is acceptable, but as the ball gets closer to the weak side wall (five feet or so), this becomes much harder, and if very close to the wall, impossible. However, you should realize that the more you "run around" your weak side, the less confidence and competence you will have on that side. In addition, you are going to leave yourself out of position quite often, and will have to do more running to get back in position. Some players adhere to the philosophy of using their weak side primarily for defensive shots (especially from the back court), but to become a really complete player this is not the best advice to follow. All it will take on your part is a little more concentrated effort and extra practice with your weak side, and you will be a much stronger and more capable player for your efforts.

COURT POSITION AND SHOT ANTICIPATION

The beginning paddle or racquetball player can do a lot to aid his success and perfection of the game by practicing good shot anticipation and court position. The ideal position when your opponent is hitting his shot is in the center of the court and just behind the short line. However, you will not always be able to get ot that position in one move, and should not even try. The most important thing is that you do not get caught off balance by trying to go too far; work your way to the position a shot at a time.

Remember, the most important thing to watch is the ball, and then your opponent. When playing, try not to place your opponent directly between you and the ball or shot, in order to avoid screening or blocking your view of the ball. Try to place yourself in a position where you can watch the shot, or at least see the ball, and from which you can move quickly and most directly to your shot. Figs. 7.8 and 7.9 illustrate two of these positions.

In paddle or racquetball, as in most games where your opponent is in front of you, it is much easier to see and watch your opponent and the ball. However, when your opponent is behind you (as he will be a great deal of the time), it is imperative that you do watch him, and don't just stare at the front wall while waiting for the ball. In order to do this safely, you may either raise the elbow of the arm on the side of the shot and look underneath that arm to follow the shot, or you may raise the arm on the

Figure 7.8 Position of players with front man watching play while ready for shot

Figure 7.9 Position of players with back man watching play while ready for shot

side of the shot, spread the fingers of that hand and watch the shot through them. (Figs. 7.10 and 7.11.)

The purpose of either method is to shield the eyes and face from being hit by the ball and to enable you to watch your opponent and his ensuing shot. This will also enable you to become more effective at hitting fly kills and passing shots.

When your opponent is behind you, try to position yourself so that his best open shot will be made to your strongest side, and attempt to give him only one or two possible shots, rather than the whole court to work

Figure 7.10 The correct method of looking under the arm to watch play in rear of court

Figure 7.11 The correct method of looking through the fingers to watch play in rear of court

with. Figs. 7.12 and 7.13 illustrate this. Remember that more defensive shots will come from behind you (unless you set your opponent up), and more kills and passes from in front of you. Plan accordingly.

Watch your opponent to see if he gives his intentions away prior to his shots. How does he stand for particular shots and which are his strongest and weakest shots? A big, fast arm swing will mean that the ball will be hit much harder than a short, slow swing. Watch his arm, elbow and paddle or racquethead to determine angle and spin of shots. Does he step directly toward the direction of his shots or off to one side? Anything you can do to anticipate his shots will strengthen your game.

Figure 7.12 Players positioned so that the front man is in a good position to wait for return

Figure 7.13 The front man is in a good position to watch and wait for return

There are a number of things you can do to increase your own movement efficiency. Just prior to your opponent's shot, take a small hop or jump. This will enable you to start much faster than from a flat-footed stance. Some players like to take a small step toward the direction they think the shot is going (step with the foot on that side of the court), and even if they are wrong this will get them started moving faster. The best advice for moving is, do not wait until the ball rebounds off the front wall; you must try to determine where the shot is heading prior to that and move accordingly. When a kill shot is hit, you must automatically move up. When a lob or ceiling shot is hit you must move back quickly so that you will not have to scramble recklessly at the last minute. As you run for a shot do not overrun it but try, if you can, to stop a step or so away from the contact point so that you can stride into the shot, and thereby increase its effectiveness.

Remember that the paddle or racquet increases your reach if you are used to handball and decreases it if you are a tennis player. Learn to conserve your energy by not going all-out in vain attempts at impossible saves. If you are totally tired out by the end of the first game, you are in trouble. By the same token try not to run at full speed for all your shots but start slowly until you can determine the court position you want and the exact speed and direction of your opponent's shot.

PSYCHOLOGY OF PLAY

Once you achieve a certain level of competency and skill the game of paddle or racquetball becomes, as most other individual and dual sports do, psychological. The thinking part of the game begins to make up anywhere from 70 to 90 percent of the game. What is meant by this, and how can it affect you and your game?

The thinking player will win far more matches than the nonthinker. If your opponent has little stamina and endurance it would be wise to run him and wear him down quickly. Learn to pace yourself. Play your best shots and protect your weaknesses. Try to set yourself up by creating patterns of play, and also try to determine your opponent's pattern of play: what are his favorite shots and from where, etc. If you are winning using a particular strategy, do not change it until your opponent can beat it, or until it fails you. Do not force a losing strategy; rather, try another method, but remember that one or two shots is not a good indicator.

It is as important for you to play the game mentally as it is physically. Mentally picture your shots and the court, so that you are prepared for them. Do not let missed shots or lost points (no matter how easy) bother you. Play each point separately. Getting mad and upset can only serve to ruin the rest of your game. Temper, talk and tantrums have no place on the paddle or racquetball court. They are not good for your game and they will certainly ruin your opponent's game, probably to the point where he will not want to play with you again.

Paddle and racquetball are games of finesse, skill, and agility, and not body contact. Sometimes hinders are unavoidable; make sure you do not take unfair advantage of this rule, and do not call hinders on shots you have no chance of reaching. Review the rules (Chapter 3). Remember, even though winning is more fun than losing, it is only a game and therefore designed for exercise, enjoyment and interaction. Play it with these objectives in mind and you will probably win even more.

Doubles

8

The game of doubles is a very different one from that of singles. The fact that you may be a good singles player does not necessarily mean you will also be a good doubles player. Two average singles players who can work well together will probably make a better doubles team than two better singles players who cannot work together. The secret of success in doubles lies in teamwork. A good doubles team can be compared to a good marriage. Both partners must work together, cooperate with one another, learn to know each other's strengths and weaknesses and enjoy working with one another. There can be no success for you in doubles if you try to make all the shots, or if you blame your partner for every shot he misses or sets up. There is no room in the game of doubles for criticism or hard feelings. Talk over strategy, strengths, weaknesses and position prior to or after the matches, or during practice sessions. Doubles is a fast game, and because of the number of players on the court it requires more precise shots, more careful planning, and more courtesy. The game of doubles, when played correctly, will really give you a feeling of accomplishment for yourself and your partner.

COURT POSITION

Because there are two of you playing together, you will have to divide up the court for the best possible coverage. When you do this you must keep in mind your own strengths and weaknesses, strong sides, speed and endurance, and general court savvy. There are a number of ways you and your partner can split the court. You will find that some leave too many open spots, i.e., the up and back method (Fig. 8.1) and the diagonal method (Fig. 8.2). The best way for your team to decide on the positions to use is to experiment. Do not be afraid to use an unorthodox method, because you may have success with it.

Perhaps the best, most time-tested method used by most better teams is the side by side position. Fig. 8.3 illustrates this. When using this method, divide the court down the center from the front wall to the back wall, with each taking a half.

When two right or left handers are playing, you must decide who will play the left and right sides, just as you must do if one of you is left and the other right-handed. There are many opinions as to who should play which side, and again, the best way for you to decide is to experiment.

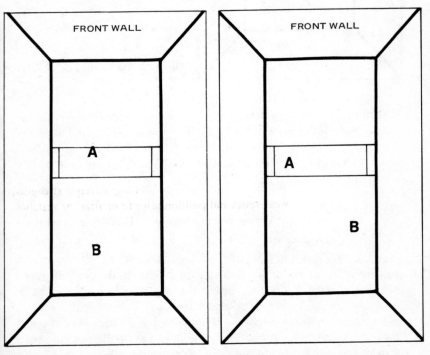

Figure 8.1 The up and back method. (A) the front court (B) the back court

Figure 8.2 The diagonal method. A and B are always on a diagonal from each other

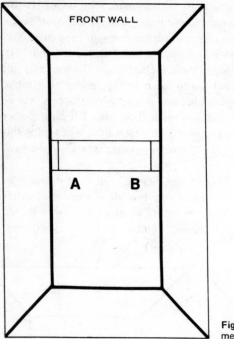

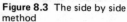

Figure 8.3 The side by side method

If both of you are right-handed you may try the stronger player on the left side and give him more of the back court to cover. (Fig. 8.4.) By doing this he will be hitting his forehand more often and his opponent will have fewer backhands. If both players are left-handed the opposite of this would apply. (Fig. 8.5.)

The Left Side

This side (for right-handers) would be the dominant side of the court. (Fig. 8.4.) The player in this half of the court would end up taking perhaps 80 percent of the shots. He should be the stronger of the two players and have better stamina and endurance. The advantage he has, of course, is being able to use his strong forehand for many shots his partner would ordinarily hit with his backhand. The ideal court position for this man is shown in Fig. 8.4. He will not always be able to get to this position, but it should serve as a guide for him. The left side player needs to have a good backhand as well as a good forehand so that the opposition cannot take advantage of the left wall and corner.

Since the left side player will normally play a bit deeper than his partner, he should not get caught too far up in the front court on a play (unless he is executing a kill shot to end the rally), but should try to get back to his ideal position after making a front court shot. By doing this, his opponents cannot take advantage of him with a passing shot, thereby putting his partner at a great disadvantage.

Another duty that should be assumed by the left side player is that of quarterback. On balls hit between him and his partner, he should be the one responsible for calling whose shot it is. Remember, if two left-handers are playing together the opposite of what is written above will be true.

The Right Side

The person who plays the right side (if both are right-handed) has a very difficult assignment; not so much from a physical standpoint, but from a psychological one. Since the left side player will handle about 80

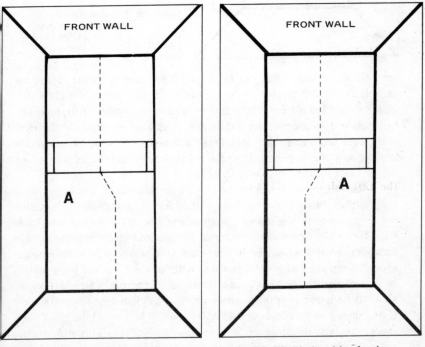

Figure 8.4 The ideal position for the righthanded left side player

Figure 8.5 The ideal position for the lefthanded right side player

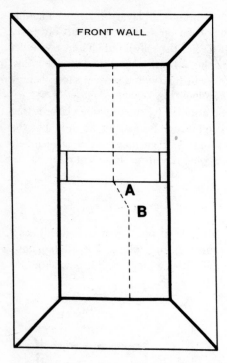

FRONT WALL

A
B

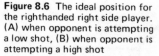

Figure 8.6 The ideal position for the righthanded right side player. (A) when opponent is attempting a low shot, (B) when opponent is attempting a high shot

percent of the shots, this can be a very frustrating position. There are exceptions to this if, for example, the right side player's backhand is stronger than his forehand, and that of his partner as well. This, however, will not be too common an occurrence. The ideal position for the right side player is closer to the short line (Fig. 8.6 A) when the opponents are attempting a kill shot and further toward the back court (Fig. 8.6 B) when they are attempting a defensive shot.

Just because you will not be playing as many shots, do not shy away from hitting your share of the balls, and do not make the mistake of standing too close to the right wall. Doing this will force you to use your backhand too often, and will also increase the pressure on your partner. The exception to this would be if your backhand was one of your stronger shots. When the ball is hit down the center of the court and your partner is in good position and has a good forehand, it is better to let him take the shot. If he is not in good position and you are, it is best if you take the shot. Since you have less court ot cover and will be toward the front cover more, you will therefore be in a position to hit more kills and attempt more fly kills and passes, so it is important that you work on developing these particular shots.

When your opponent is behind or in front of you and is attempting a shot, the same rules apply in doubles as in singles. Do not let him block your view of the shot and ball, and do not put yourself in an impossible position for retrieval of the shot. When you are in front of your opponent, watch him make the shot, and do not give him too much court to work with or allow him to hit to your weakness. Remember that you and your partner are a team, and you must work that way if you expect to play well together.

LEFT-HANDER

If one member of your team is left-handed and the other right-handed, you will want to use a different strategy than if you both favor the same hand. Split the court down the middle (Fig. 8.7), and then decide if you want your forehands down the middle or on the outsides. More points are scored down the sides, so it is probably a good idea to put your forehands

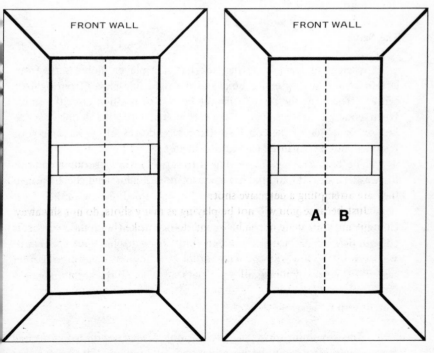

Figure 8.7 Court division for a lefthanded and righthanded doubles team

Figure 8.8 The player with the stronger forehand (A) in a left-righthanded doubles team, standing closer to the center

on the outside. If the player with the stronger forehand stands a bit closer to the center of the court (Fig. 8.8), he will be able to use his forehand on many of the shots down the center of the court.

Since your weak spot will then be down the middle, the best strategy is to let the man with the strongest backhand hit the shot if he is in position. This will most often apply to the front court, because usually one of you will be able to step around the ball in the back court and use the stronger forehand shot. You may want to experiment with your forehands down the middle if your opponents are having trouble keeping the ball down the sides, or if your backhands are both very strong.

PLAY STRATEGY

The playing strategy for doubles in paddle or racquetball is the same as it is for singles: hit a kill shot or other offensive shot when you have the opportunity, otherwise hit a defensive shot and work your way into the offensive position.

The Serve

When your team is serving, the left side player should serve from left to center in the service box, and the right side player from right of center. This way the server will not be out of position after the serve. When your partner is serving make sure you stand in the doubles service box on your side of the court, so that if you do get hit by the serve your team will not be penalized (see rules, Chapter 3).

The best strategy for serving is to serve to the weaker man and to his weaker side. If you find a weak spot do not let up and change just to be fair to his partner. Against a left and right handed team with their forehands to the outside, try low, hard serves down the center, or a low drive that angles into the center of the court. Experiment with types of serves to both partners and to various points in the court to find your opponents' weaknesses. Following your serve, make sure both you and your partner watch it closely and are ready to put the shot away on the next hit.

The Return Of Service

When returning serve you have one objective in mind: to get the ball back. If the serve is not particularly strong, attempt an offensive shot, but if the serve is strong, use a defensive return. Again, direct your return (if possible) at the weaker of your opponents and to his weakest side. If the serve is hit down the middle of the court, the receiver with the strongest return should hit the ball, and often this will be the left side player (if both players are right handed). While the receiver returns the shot, his partner should move toward the short line, making sure he does not get in the way of the return. The ideal back court positions for receiving service are illustrated in Figs. 8.9, 8.10, and 8.11.

Remember when receiving service to be alert for the possibility of a fly kill or a fly pass in order that you may end the rally as quickly as possible. The longer the ball is in play, the more opportunities your opponents will have to win the point. Do not be afraid to talk to one another to help your efforts. Remember, you are a team and must work together.

Playing Strategy

The fact that there are four players instead of only two on the court imposes some situations which must be considered if you are going to be a successful team. Your shots must become more accurate, you will have to hit the ball harder, and you will not be able to use the passing shot as often as in singles. Remember that two players (partners) can cover the court pretty well, and will be able to reach most shots, especially soft ones. Get together with your partner and discuss your strategy. Plan a sequence of shots if you can and see how close you can come to executing that plan.

Figure 8.9 Court position for receiving serve when both players are righthanded

Figure 8.10 Court position for receiving serve when both players are lefthanded

Figure 8.11 Court position for receiving serve when one player is righthanded (player on right) and one player is lefthanded.

Decide what the weak spots in your opponents' game are, and try to really exploit them.

One type of strategy, which is also used in handball and squash (when your opponents are a stronger team), is to hit everything to the stronger player in hopes of tiring him out quickly and thereby increasing your chances of winning. Figure out what the weak spots are in your own game, and see how well you can disguise them and compensate for them. Attempt to kill the shot any time you have a good chance. Review the section on kill shots and their placement and remember to work the ball away from your opponents. Figs. 8.12 through 8.15 illustrate some of the kill shot situations. If both of your opponents are up, the two-wall passing shot can be effective. (Fig. 8.16.)

When using the three-wall defensive shot, remember to hit it hard, and if your opponents start cutting it off before it reaches the back court, aim closer to the front wall and the rebound will be different. Make sure your ceiling and lob shots are hit softly enough so they do not rebound off the back wall and set up your opponents.

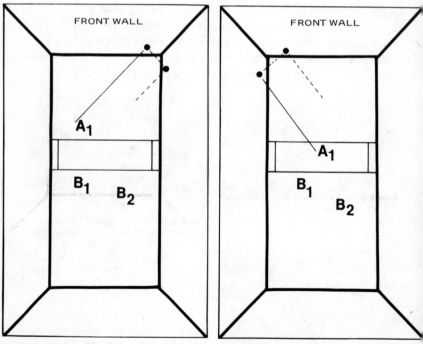

Figure 8.12 Right inside corner kill with right side opponent back

Figure 8.13 Left outside corner kill with right side opponent back

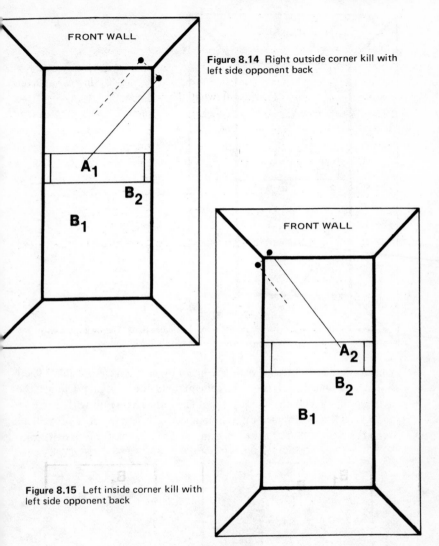

Figure 8.14 Right outside corner kill with left side opponent back

Figure 8.15 Left inside corner kill with left side opponent back

Try to take advantage of any weak shot hit by your opponent, and think while playing. Doubles is a game where you must move constantly, because if you do not, you will probably lose. Force yourself, especially when your partner is either hitting or waiting to hit, to move into a good position. The rule in tennis doubles is get your first serve in; not necessarily a really fast, hard one, but one that is placed well and will force a weak return. The same rule applies to paddle and racquetball. When serving,

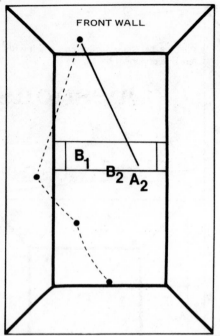

FRONT WALL

B₁

B₂ A₂

Figure 8.16 Two-wall pass with both opponents up

you are on the offense and want to remain there as long as possible. Therefore work on control, spin, placement, and then speed. The game of doubles offers you the unique experience of teaming up with a partner, good friend, acquaintance or complete stranger; and pitting your skill and expertise against that of another team. Make it an enjoyable experience.

Figure 8.17 Follow-through of a lob shot

Questions
for
Evaluation

1.   The strings of the racquet allow the player to put more spin on the ball. What types of spin are possible and how do they effect the direction, bounce and rebound of the ball?

2.   What do you feel are the advantages or disadvantages of racquetball versus paddleball?

3.   Why is it important to develop your backhand as well as your forehand?

4.   There are progressions that can be followed in learning and perfecting each skill. Do you feel theses are important, and if so, why?

5.   What is the real value of training for racquetball or paddleball? How would you train?

6.   There are a number of methods of serving in either game. Which do you prefer, and why?

7.   What is the importance of having more than one serve?

8.   Describe your immediate objectives if you are in each of the following positions.
     a.   server
     b.   receiver
     c.   during play and on the offense
     d.   during play and on the defense

9.   The lob shot requires a delicate touch in order to be executed well. Is there value in learning this shot and if so, what is it?

10.   When playing singles you should strive to pace yourself. What is meant by this, and how will it affect your game?

11.   What is the purpose of a game plan or strategy? Give an example of how you would devise or envision such a plan.

12.   Is it a good idea to over-protect your weak side? Explain your answer.

13.   What roles do court position and shot anticipation play in a match? How would you go about accomplishing good position?

14.   How can the psychology of play affect your game? Your opponent's?

15.   In the game of doubles, which formation do you prefer, why, and what are the advantages or disadvantages?

16.   What, other than involving four players instead of two, makes doubles a different game than singles? Which do you prefer, and why?

17.   What are some of the playing strategies for doubles?

18.   Why do you enjoy racquetball or paddleball? Which do you prefer, and why?

19.   If you do not care for either game, why?

Suggested Readings

Allsen, P. E., and Witbeck, A. *Paddleball.* Dubuque, Iowa: Wm. C. Brown Co., 1972.

Godleski, E. E. "Paddleball For Girls." *Journal of Health Physical Education and Recreation.* 39:62.

Kozare, A. J., Trambeau, R. J. and Riskey, E. N. *Beginning Paddleball.* Belmont, Calif.: Wadsworth Pub. Co., 1967.

Larson, C. and Wickstrom, R. *Racquetball and Paddleball Fundamentals.* Columbus, Ohio: C. E. Merrill Publishing Co., 1972.

Levin, D. "Great Mano a Raqueta: Muehleisen-Haber Match." *Sports Illustrated* 36:22-4.

Official Paddleball Rules. National Paddleball Association, Intramural Sports Building, Ann Arbor, Michigan 48104, 1970.

Official IRA Racquetball Rules. International Racquetball Association, 4101 Dempster Street, Skokie, Illinois 60076, 1972.

Racquetball Magazine. Chicago, Ill. Published by the International Racquetball Association and the National Paddleball Association.

Weil, J. "Stars Battle at Memphis for World Racquetball Championships." *Tennis,* 8:40-41.

Student/Teacher Instructional Objectives

Comments on the Use of the Student/Teacher Evaluation Forms

The forms which follow were designed to be used in a variety of instructional settings. Preplanning and organization are necessary for these devices to be used as effectively as possible. The purpose of evaluation is for gauging how well the course objectives are accomplished. That is, evaluation will indicate the progress and the extent to which learning has occurred.

Although the learner *must do his own learning*, the teacher's role is to guide and to direct learning experiences and to provide for appropriate measurement procedures. The charts which follow have been constructed to place primary responsibility on the individual student for estimating progress and indicating areas which need work. It may not be either necessary or desirable to use all the materials provided here in a given teaching learning situation. The instructor and the student should work together to select the materials most appropriate for the course.

It must be remembered that sufficient time for practice and study must be provided if the individual is to perfect his skills as well to accrue knowledge and to develop understanding. The time available may not be adequate for *all* students to demonstrate acceptable levels of skill performance. The instructor may wish to supplement the evaluation devices with a written test covering analysis of performance, procedures, and rules. (Sample tests will be available in a separate instructor's manual covering the entire Goodyear Physical Activities series.) The written test provides an opportunity for the student to demonstrate his knowledge and understanding of the skill even though his actual skill might be less than desired. Final evaluation for grading purposes should take into account a number of variables which may have an influence on individual performance.

STUDENT	FOREHAND	TEACHER
_____	Accuracy	_____
_____	Power	_____
_____	Speed	_____
_____	Spin	_____
_____	Top	_____
_____	Under	_____
_____	Slice	_____
_____	Back Court	_____
_____	Front Court	_____
_____	Straight Kill	_____
_____	Corner Kill	_____
_____	Back Court Kill	_____
_____	Straight Pass	_____
_____	Two Wall Pass	_____
_____	Back Court Pass	_____
_____	Lob	_____
_____	Front Court	_____
_____	Back Court	_____
_____	Ceiling Shot	_____
_____	Front Court	_____
_____	Back Court	_____
_____	Overhead Shot	_____

_____ TOTAL EFFICIENCY _____

STUDENT	BACKHAND	TEACHER
_____	Accuracy	_____
_____	Power	_____
_____	Speed	_____

PADDLEBALL AND RACQUETBALL: Student/Teacher Instructional Objectives

STUDENT		TEACHER
_____	Spin	_____
_____	Top	_____
_____	Under	_____
_____	Slice	_____
_____	Back Court	_____
_____	Front Court	_____
_____	Straight Kill	_____
_____	Corner Kill	_____
_____	Back Court Kill	_____
_____	Straight Pass	_____
_____	Two Wall Pass	_____
_____	Back Court Pass	_____
_____	Lob	_____
_____	Front Court	_____
_____	Back Court	_____
_____	Ceiling Shot	_____
_____	Front Court	_____
_____	Back Court	_____
_____	Overhead Shot	_____
_____	TOTAL EFFICIENCY	_____

SERVES

Power

STUDENT		TEACHER
_____	Accuracy	_____
_____	Power	_____
_____	Speed	_____
_____	Spin	_____
_____	TOTAL EFFICIENCY	_____

STUDENT	Lob	TEACHER
_____	Accuracy	_____
_____	Depth	_____
_____	Spin	_____
_____	TOTAL EFFICIENCY	_____

	"z" Serve	
_____	Accuracy	_____
_____	Power	_____
_____	Speed	_____
_____	Spin	_____
_____	TOTAL EFFICIENCY	_____

SERVICE RECEPTION

Forehand

STUDENT		TEACHER
_____	Offensive	_____
_____	Defensive	_____
_____	Accuracy	_____
_____	Depth	_____
_____	Power	_____
_____	Spin	_____
_____	Speed	_____
_____	Lob	_____
_____	Volley	_____
_____	Kill	_____
_____	3-Wall	_____
_____	Pass	_____
_____	Cross Court	_____
_____	Straight	_____
_____	TOTAL EFFICIENCY	_____

Class _____

Student _____

Teacher _____

Date _____

STUDENT	Backhand	TEACHER
_____	Offensive	_____
_____	Defensive	_____
_____	Accuracy	_____
_____	Depth	_____
_____	Power	_____
_____	Spin	_____
_____	Speed	_____
_____	Lob	_____
_____	Volley	_____
_____	Kill	_____
_____	3-Wall	_____
_____	Pass	_____
_____	Cross Court	_____
_____	Straight	_____
_____	TOTAL EFFICIENCY	_____

TROUBLE SHOTS

Back Wall Kill

STUDENT		TEACHER
_____	Accuracy	_____
_____	Power	_____
_____	Speed	_____
_____	Spin	_____
_____	TOTAL EFFICIENCY	_____

Back Corner Kill

STUDENT		TEACHER
_____	Accuracy	_____
_____	Power	_____
_____	Speed	_____
_____	Spin	_____
_____	TOTAL EFFICIENCY	_____

Class _____

Student _____

Teacher _____

Date _____

STUDENT

SINGLES GENERAL
PLAYING STRATEGY

TEACHER

Offensive _____

_____ Defensive _____

_____ TOTAL EFFICIENCY _____

DOUBLES GENERAL
PLAYING STRATEGY

_____ Team Player _____

_____ Offensive _____

_____ Defensive _____

_____ TOTAL EFFICIENCY _____

Class _____

Student _____

Teacher _____

Date _____

NOTES